GUNFLINT:

The Trail, The People, The Stories

by John Henricksson

Adventure Publications
Cambridge, Minnesota

Dedication

For Luke, a little boy with a brand new world.

Book and cover design by Jonathan Norberg

10 9 8 7 6 5 4 3

Copyright 2003 by John Henricksson
Published by Adventure Publications
An imprint of AdventureKEEN
(800) 678-7006
www.adventurepublications.net
Printed in the U.S.A.
ISBN: 978-1-59193-310-6

Table of Contents

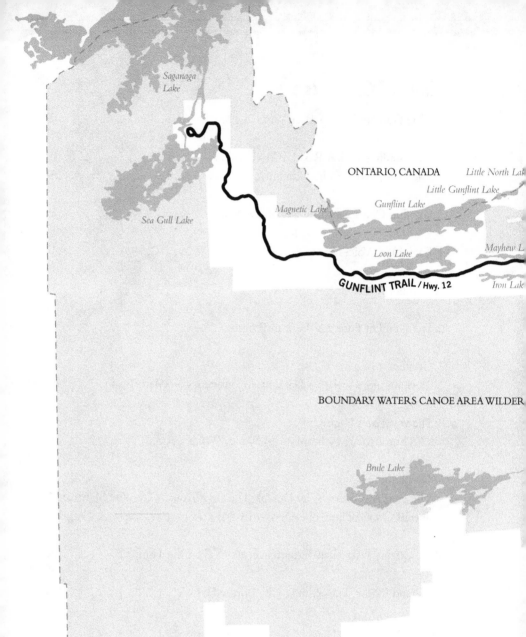

Saganaga
Lake

ONTARIO, CANADA   Little North Lak

Little Gunflint Lake

Gunflint Lake

Magnetic Lake

Sea Gull Lake

Loon Lake   Mayhew L.

GUNFLINT TRAIL / Hwy. 12   Iron Lak

BOUNDARY WATERS CANOE AREA WILDER

Brule Lake

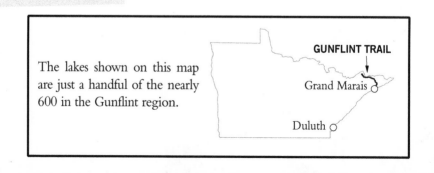

The lakes shown on this map
are just a handful of the nearly
600 in the Gunflint region.

GUNFLINT TRAIL

Grand Marais

Duluth

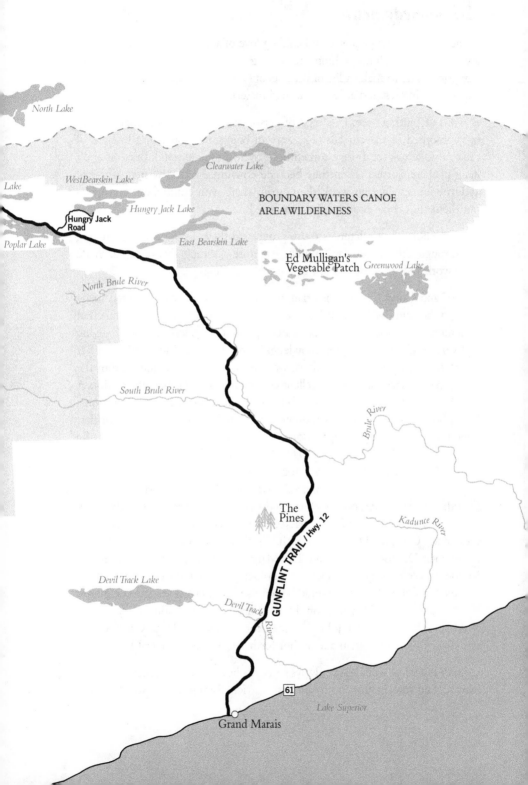

Acknowledgments

Armed with the pre-requisite and abiding love of a landscape, the best way for a writer to approach researching and writing the cultural and natural history of a region, is first to make a list of those people who have the most knowledge, experience, interest and access to needed material.

A word of caution here: This type of person will often be an academic; very busy, absorbed in the current task, wary of being misquoted, and because of their professional vocabulary, sometimes easy to misunderstand. But one must hang in there. Persist. When they become convinced of the writer's sincerity and true interest in their work, they usually share with enthusiasm. And without them, the whole project is in deep weeds.

My first effort was to determine this group, and they never failed me, guiding me through their particular Gunflint expertise, forming the sturdy, accurate framework and structure the rest of the material clings to.

Author and Cook County historian, the late Willis Raff, who devoted many years to the study of Gunflint history, has been not only a primary source but a mentor; first among equals. Forest Ecologist, Chel Anderson; patient, giving and very bright, her scientific knowledge of the forest and its family, and her ability to communicate it to others, was fundamental to my quest. From the U.S. Forest Service there was excellent cooperation and reliable information. A list of individuals would be long, but outstanding were: Superior National Forest Supervisor, Jim Sanders, Gunflint and Tofte District Ranger, Jo Barnier; Superior National Forest Supervisory Archaeologist, Gordon Peters, (ret.); the current supervisor, Archaeologist David Woodward, who is also coordinator of the USFS Heritage Resources Program; Bill Ross, Archaeologist for the Ontario Ministry of Citizenship, Culture and Recreation; David Zentner, Duluth conservationist, outdoorsman and past National President of the Izaak Walton League; Dr. David Zumeta, Executive Director of the Minnesota Forest Resources Council; Dr. Peter Reich, Professor of Forestry, University of Minnesota; Dr. John Tester and Dr. Margaret Davis, retired University of Minnesota ecologists; Janet Green, ornithologist, author and past director of the National Audubon Society. I would be remiss if I did not credit the late Miron Heinselman for my reliance on his seminal work, The Boundary Waters Wilderness Ecosystem, Dr. John C. Green, for Geology on Display, and Shirley Peruniak, Ontario historian and author for her Quetico Provincial Park.

County historical societies are always treasure chests for those seeking accurate, hard to find information from the past. Patricia Zankman, the dynamic and resourceful director of the Cook County Historical Society, who was busy creating a computerized data base from the thousands of yellowing documents in her care always found time to locate exactly what I was looking for. Sue Kerfoot, neighbor, ex-resort operator and regional history buff, has the most complete files of Gunflint stories, unpublished manuscripts, old clippings, oral history tapes, correspondence and firsthand knowledge of Gunflint "people" history. She graciously gave me access to all of it.

Old Timers (always the best source for intriguing area information) Fred Dell, Orv Gilmore, Willard Johnson, Wes Hedstrom, Justine Kerfoot, Eve Blankenburg, Ken Rusk, Betty Powell Skoog, Dick and Lou Anderson, Peggy Heston, Elinor Matsis, Catherine Lush and several others willingly shared their memories, stories and historical insights of those earlier days on The Gunflint.

Then there are the niche specialists. These are the people who have a specific expertise that is so necessary to legitimize the writer's wanderings into complex, rocky areas where it is so easy to stumble. Sometimes enthusiasm for our subject allows us to make superficial, or even hare-brained statements, and these niche specialists keep us honest.

My list of minders was a long one, but outstanding in their willingness to help were: Cook County Recorder, Dusty Nelms; Cook County Soil and Water Administrator, Rebecca Wiinanen; Gunflint region naturalists, Ken and Molly Hoffman; Northwest Ontario Railroad historian, David Battistel; canoe outfitters David Seaton and Debbie Mark; USFS Trails Coordinator Becky Spears-Bartol; Botanist for the DNR's Natural Heritage Program, Welby Smith; USFS ecologist, Wayne Russ; Joanne Hart, the elegant Minnesota poet and sole remaining resident of the Old Border Crossing on the Pigeon River; University of Minnesota Duluth Research Specialist, Bill Burgeson; Jay Anderson, the former director of the Grand Marais Art Colony; birding historian Val Cunningham; the former director of the North House Folk School, Mark Hansen; the Troll Lady, folklorist Lise Lunge-Larson and my wife Julie, whose sharp editorial eye and penchant for tidy sentences was always crucial.

Roads that dip and curve into the hills

are forest tracks where fox and bear leave scats

to mark their place. Through mist, a moose walks fast

with heavy grace, each slight twist of her path,

each step transmitted to her trailing calf.

The season's turning brings the snowy owl

who hunts the winter day on snowy wings.

From *The Village Schoolmaster* by Joanne Hart

CHAPTER 1

The Gunflint: God's Back Yard

Place names have a unique power to fascinate and they beckon the map reader to finger prowl the wild places. In northeastern Minnesota, in the deep forests and along pristine waterways, there are many of these melodic names which evoke the legends and romance of the North Country. Names like Devil Track, Flute Reed, Fishdance, Castle Danger, Lime Cloud, Hungry Jack and Gunflint. These names conjure a curiosity and wonder about the stories that created them.

Chief among these is The Gunflint—a colloquialism for the area which the U.S. Forest Service calls the Gunflint Corridor and which writer Loren Kallsen describes in his introduction to *Gunflint Territory* as "anywhere within a two day paddle of the Gunflint Trail," a useful encompassment that takes in most of Cook County, Minnesota, and a chunk of northern Ontario.

The earliest recorded name for Gunflint was *Biwanago*, a Native American word meaning flint. The current name dates back to the Fur Century when French Voyageur canoemen, Cree and Ojibwe, and the shadowy coureurs du bois, or illicit, freelance traders, traversed the region in the 1700s. Here they stopped at the long, narrow Lac Pierre a Fusil (literally, Lake of the Gun Rocks, or Gunflint) to gather chips of flint for firestones and their flintlock firearms.

From the perspective of cultural history it is a relatively new land. After the Civil War, St. Paul was the territorial capital city and Minneapolis had begun its flour milling industry. Stillwater, Mankato, Fergus Falls, Red Wing and St. Cloud were bustling, fast-growing cities, largely because their river locations gave them access to transportation and power. But there is no record of anyone at that time, white or indigenous, occupying this region of northeastern Minnesota that was to become The Gunflint. It literally has no recorded history before the Treaty of La Pointe in 1854, which opened this Native American territory to white settlement.

This arrowhead-shaped tip of Cook County has changed names considerably throughout the history of North America. It became a province of Quebec in 1774, the Northwest Territory in 1787, the Indiana Territory in 1800, the Illinois Territory in 1809, the Michigan Territory in 1818, the Wisconsin Territory in 1836 and finally was included in Minnesota's territorial status in 1849 and in the statehood grant of 1858.

Each year, thousands of canoeists paddle and portage through the two-million-acre Quetico-Superior Canoe County Wilderness. Reservations for campsites are necessary, but many canoeists camp for days without ever seeing another person.

Arguably, Cook is the most beautiful county in the state, and on the map it looks like it was pasted on as an afterthought: a sharp point of rocky, heavily forested land inserted between the 315-mile watery necklace of the Boundary Waters Canoe Area Wilderness on the northern edge, and the serrated bulk of the Sawtooth Mountains' volcanic flows surging into Lake Superior on the southern side.

The Gunflint is a national treasure of public and private land, a dense forest mosaic, rich in lakes, ponds, bogs and foaming rivers that take brawling headers down rocky chutes from the continental divide that sends water north into Hudson's Bay and south into Lake Superior.

Author and naturalist Mark (Sparky) Stensaas says, "It isn't as grand as mountains; it's more subtle and you need to learn much about it to understand its majesty."

From the air, the terrain looks rather flat and tilted, but descend a little and it becomes pleated and wrinkled into immense forest, canyons, ridges, moraines, cliffs and sills, all sculpted by prehistoric volcanic upheavals, then the wind, then the ice-scouring of the last great glacier, which retreated from here about 10,000–12,000 years ago.

Here the signature white pines tower over the narrow gravel road that was the Gunflint Trail in 1930. This entire section of the Trail was once owned by a logging company, but for some still unknown reason, these pines were never cut.

"A little messy and patchy maybe, with all the storm-downed trees and clear cuts, but from up here it still looks like God's back yard," exclaimed Old Lucas as he looked down on the Gunflint region, which had been his home for most of his 82 years, from the passenger seat of a twin-engine, white Cessna.

"When I was in the 'CCs we used to go hunting silver nuggets in those lumpy hills west of Poplar Lake," he yelled over the engine's clatter. "And over there, just under the wing. That's Whiskey Lake where Crazy Hjalmar used to have his still during Prohibition. It was up there near the new power line where the creek comes in...and look up north there at the canoes going over the portage into Round Lake. Looks like a herd of turtles with green, red and silver shells."

Lucas came here in 1938 as a member of the Civilian Conservation Corps, a semi-military program initiated by the Federal government during the Great Depression. It provided jobs in healthy outdoor settings with good barracks and mess halls for men who built roads and log and stone buildings for the state parks, fought fires, improved timber stands and built trails and portages. These men generally spruced up the area in a way that would soon draw thousands of tourists and summer cabin owners

"God, it's still beautiful country, ain't it Sandy?" marveled Lucas, turning back to his pilot. "Kind of beat up and patchy from the storm and hard used by the loggers, but most of it is still beautiful." The "storm" happened in July of 1999—known as the Big Blowdown—and flattened thousands of acres of trees in the Gunflint region with powerful straight-line winds.

Later, when they were tying the plane up at the Seagull Lake dock, Sandy asked about the changes Lucas had seen over the years.

"Well, in spite of all the blowdowns, the feel of the Gunflint hasn't really changed that much. We'll be seeing those blowdowns, log piles, snapped-off snags for years, but it's kind of exciting to see the new forest coming so fast. Whether they burn or rot, the downed trees will eventually return to soil and the whole cycle will begin again."

Gunflint Lodge

Experienced canoeists usually paddle near shore rather than out in the middle of the lake where the points, bays and islands offer a lee where they can duck out of the wind.

Back on pilot Sandy's dock, Lucas was getting into one of his expansive moods now that the plane ride was over and he had his feet under him again.

"Well, Lucas, how do you like flying?" Sandy asked.

"Pretty good, pretty good, Sandy," Lucas said. "You sure pick the bumpy roads up there though. I guess I've been prowling the woods and paddling a canoe too long to ever be much of a flier.

"I thought that cow moose on the Ida Lake portage was the best part of the trip. Remember, we were coming in kind of low over the portage and the moose was standing in an alder thicket right by the big rock. A canoe party was sitting there having their lunch and that moose couldn't have been more than a couple rods away from them, stretching her neck out and sniffing. Funny thing was they didn't have any idea there was a moose around. When they get back to the city their friends will probably ask if they saw any moose up here and they'll say, 'Nope, never saw a one.' But a moose sure saw them."

"Lucas, how come so many lakes up here have women's names?" Sandy wondered. "You were just talking about Ida Lake, and then not far away are Thelma, Clara, Ada and Sylvia Lakes. Then there's Grace, Phoebe and Beth over near the Sawbill Trail, and Polly, Christine and Helen a little to the south."

Helping himself to the coffee and doughnuts Sandy's wife Katy had brought down to the dock, Lucas grinned and explained. "Well, when this country was first surveyed and divided into townships, the government surveyors were the some of the first ones in here. In order to map what they were surveying they had to give names to the smaller, unnamed lakes they came across and most of them just penciled in their own, or friends, names like Jerry, Don and Ross near Brule Lake and Jake, Morgan and Carl over near the Misquah Hills. When they ran out of them, they often used their girlfriends' names, and you know those guys, most of 'em had lots of girlfriends. But sometimes they even ran out of those names so they used other stuff like Ed Mulligan, the Gunflint's first forester, up in that country northwest of Greenwood Lake. By the way, he was the guy who first laid out the Sawbill Trail, you know.

"Ed was surveying that region in 1885 and he ran across a slew of nameless little lakes in there so he called them Carrot, Parsnip, Potato, Cucumber, Bean, Onion and Celery and the area became known as Ed Mulligan's Vegetable Patch. Lot of the lakes have Native American names, of course, but they were known long before any of us got here."

"Funny things about those names," Lucas went on. "The old stories seem to stick, no matter what. The Kadunce River story is a good example of the way names get mixed up but never lost. It is really named for Joe Kadunce, an old Ojibwe, who lived on the river, but early white settlers called it Diarrhea River as a warning to people not to drink its water. There still is a Diarrhea Creek coming into the Kadunce far up toward its headwaters.

"Later on, I guess some local people didn't think that was a very attractive name for their river, so they renamed it after Joe Kadunce. Then the confusion really started. Somehow the legend that grew up around the river had it that Kadunce was the Ojibwe word for diarrhea, but Shannon Crossbear tells me that just isn't true. Still that legend lives on, always will I suppose. Seems most folks prefer a good story to an accurate one and they seem to like that 'Diarrhea River' story."

Many of the stories touch on the long history of people who had come into the Gunflint region over the past 150 years, prospecting, trapping, logging, fishing or escaping disastrous national events such as depressions and financial panics like those in 1857, 1873 and 1893. Some saw an escape from overwhelming problems, or a need to stay a step ahead of the law and felt the need for new beginnings in a new country. Freedom and independence are classic motivations for emigration, and have been part of the demographic history of many remote areas of the nation.

The very first arrivals, who came shortly after the territory was opened to white settlement in 1854, were mostly fortune seekers—mineral prospectors, fur traders and land speculators. But from the Civil War on through two World Wars and the Great Depression many came for another chance.

Early homes, many belonging to immigrant Norwegian fishermen and farmers, clung to the rugged shore of Lake Superior and sprawled over Maple Hill, the beautiful hillside neighborhood above town that was beginning to blossom into Grand Marais, but it wasn't long before other arrivals began looking beyond the hill to the forest and lakes of the upcountry.

At the turn of the century, after a brief flurry of iron mining in the Gunflint Lake area, logging revived activity in the Gunflint region. But after World War I, it became apparent that the area's economic future lay in the burgeoning tourist industry as the automobile made the area accessible to sportsmen and vacationers.

The resort business on the Gunflint Trail had its beginnings before the turn of the century when, in the late 1890s, Hans Gilbertson built a few crude cabins on the South Brule and Assinika Creek near Greenwood Lake. He rented these out to moose hunters and made about $800 a year on this operation, big money at a time when the country was in a deep depression. Hans also provided a shuttle service from town by ox cart.

Accessibility was, of course, the big problem. By 1900, there was a trail along the North Shore Drive, albeit only a stagecoach and sleigh road from Duluth to Grand Marais, which was also a winter dogsled mail route. Two large Lake Superior passenger steamers, the *Dixon* and the *Bon Ami*, regularly brought tourists to Grand Marais and the Gunflint as did the larger and more luxurious *America*, which later replaced the *Dixon*.

In 1911, Charlie Boostrom, the father of the modern day Gunflint region resort business, came into the country and in many ways the Gunflint would never be the same. He was a restless man of boundless energy, many talents and a wonderful imagination. In 1915, he built a small rental cabin on Clearwater Lake near mid-Trail and called it "Clearwater Lodge." By 1918, he had built the present Clearwater Lodge, the first real resort in the area: an imposing, two-story structure of native white pine logs, which is still operating and has been placed on the National Register of Historic Places.

courtesy Linda Tvedt and Mark Marchino

Charlie Boostrom and his dog Babe stand outside their cabin, which Charlie built in 1918 and where he and Petra lived in while Clearwater lodge was under construction. It seemed Charlie could build anything, but he especially loved to design and build fireplaces. Cabins and resorts all over the Gunflint region still feature Boostrom fireplaces.

Clearwater Lodge, which Charlie Boostrom built, opened in 1926. It is the largest original whole log structure in Minnesota and is the only building in the Gunflint region to be recognized by the National Register of Historic Places.

He had a successful fur and logging business, built beautiful stone fireplaces and guided fishermen and hunters, but his adventuresome nature sometimes led him into more unusual enterprises, such as the reindeer ranching business he started in 1930, which provided reindeer (domesticated caribou), a sleigh, Santa Claus (Charlie) and two elves for community Christmas parades throughout the region. Author Helen White recalls that adventure in *The Tale of a Comet:*

Charlie had built a big corral at Clearwater, hired Joe Thomas, an Ojibwe from Grand Portage, as sled builder and herder for the reindeer which were bought originally from an Alaska company. One late summer day in 1933, the reindeer kicked down the corral and disappeared into the woods. Joe Thomas tried to chase some across Clearwater Lake in a canoe, but they were never seen again, except for one that showed up in Tofte a year later with a bell and red ribbon around its neck.

By the end of the Roaring Twenties there were several fine resorts in the area, many of which have burned and been rebuilt, and are still operating in their second or third reincarnations. By the end of that decade there were Hungry Jack, Greenwood and Gunflint on their eponymous lakes, Camp Rockwood and Bear Cub on Poplar Lake, Seagull Lodge, Windigo Point and Quiet Cove—now the mainland facility of the Wilderness Canoe Base—on Seagull Lake.

The Roaring Twenties were days of affluence for some in America and The Gunflint was a fishing vacation destination for the rich and famous. Babe Ruth, Jack Dempsey and writer Ring Lardner came up to the Gunflint to fish Clearwater Lake for lake trout from Naniboujou, their club on the North

Shore. Writers Sinclair Lewis, Robert Page Lincoln and F. Scott Fitzgerald also visited the mid-Trail region then. The Weyerhauser brothers, baseball commissioner Kennesaw Mountain Landis, U.S. Labor Secretary Frances Perkins, the doctors Mayo, and later, U.S. Attorney General Herbert Brownell, all brought their families to Gateway Hungry Jack Lodge where Duncan Hines, a frequent guest, used to snitch items from Sue Gapen's menu for his recipe books. A hostess with a flair for creative details, Sue always had the waitstaff pick the largest fresh thimbleberry leaves from bushes near the lodge to be used as placemats for every meal.

What allowed the affluence at first to trickle and then flow into the heart of the Gunflint itself was the main artery knows as The Gunflint Trail.

The trailhead in Grand Marais.

In 1932, the Gunflint region was fast becoming a favorite family vacation spot and widely known for its excellent fishing. The Trail was only about 25 feet wide and was so full of hills and sharp curves that the county felt it necessary to erect an overhead sign to warn motorists to slow down and drive safely

CHAPTER 2

The Gunflint Trail: A Road to Yesterday

The Gunflint Trail begins on the Lake Superior North Shore at the town of Grand Marais, rises over the ancient remains of the volcanic Sawtooth Mountains, then wanders 56 miles in a northwesterly direction through the Superior National Forest to its terminus—a canoe-landing water which combines Gull Lake, the Seagull River and Lake Saganaga.

The first Gunflint Trail was a narrow wagon road called the Rove Lake Road in 1875 that started in Grand Marais, angled off northeast at Milepost 24—now the Hungry Jack Road—and went around Clearwater and Daniels Lakes, eventually to Rove Lake and Henry Mayhew's trading post. It didn't find its present configuration to Gunflint Lake until 1886 when iron was discovered at the west end of the lake (by Mayhew). The fact that at this time Mayhew was the first chairman of the Cook County Board undoubtedly helped with the county's decision to improve and extend the road from Milepost 24 to the new Mayhew Iron Range at Gunflint Lake, and abandon the road to Rove Lake.

Henry Mayhew, the acknowledged First Citizen of Cook County, came here from Martha's Vineyard where his Mayflower family had lived for 100 years. According to author Willis Raff in *Pioneers in the Wilderness,* "Mayhew was the single individual responsible for the development of Grand Marais and the Gunflint Road."

Before coming to the Gunflint region in 1870, he had prospected for gold on the Vermilion range with his old friend Henry Eames, the state geologist. Mayhew owned much of the harbor land in Grand Marais and along the shore. He also owned a general merchandise store in town, had mining claims throughout the county, was very active in state and local politics and was the man who hacked the first Gunflint Trail out of the wilderness. Although it was called a wagon road, it wasn't much more than a rough hiking trail then, and soon men were following it into the wilderness.

Closer to a large polar bear population than to southwest Minnesota, and the first of three surfaced roads between it and the North Pole, the Gunflint Trail was described by writer Mark Albey as "tunneling through the wilderness like a green mine."

Following the Trail back through the century is a fascinating journey of discovery in the company of men who shaped this region which Maren Scott, in her *Boundary Waters Guide* calls "a place of history, of sweating men and their dreams."

Cook County Historical Society

The first trail from Grand Marais to Gunflint Lake was little more than a wagon road. Sensing a tourist boom after World War I when automobile traffic had become common and a North Shore Drive had been constructed, the county began rebuilding and surfacing the Gunflint Trail in 1924.

After Mayhew engineered the change in the Trail that took it to Gunflint Lake, the Trail remained a narrow path over which horses, oxen and men with heavily loaded packs struggled summer and winter. Work on it progressed slowly as the county had only enough money and will to spend $300 to $600 at a time to clear and build a few more miles each year. Then in September of 1893, the *Grand Marais Herald* editor was proudly able to write: "There is now a good road all the way from Grand Marais to Gunflint."

There must have been great excitement and optimism among the population of this rugged landscape at the end of the Gunflint Trail at this time. There was a promising iron mine, a railroad and three thriving small towns in the bush. One was the town of Gunflint, with a post office and a polling place at the narrows between Gunflint and Magnetic Lakes. A second was Leeblain, a town of about 200 at the end of Oven Bay on the Canadian side of Gunflint Lake named for Arthur Lee and Hugh Blain, Toronto bankers who were responsible for much of the financing of the Canadian segment of the railroad. And there was Gunflint City, a mining town about three miles west of the Lake near the site of the test pits and mine shafts. Not even today is the population as large at the end of the Gunflint Trail as it was at the end of the 1800s.

Within a few years, both the mine and the American section of the railroad failed, although spurs carried logs for several more years, and the whole economy collapsed primarily because of some financial shenanigans, the ore's skimpy quality and quantity, and the development of the mother lodes of the Mesabi, Cayuna and Vermillion ranges 150 miles to the west.

The Gunflint Trail name has no known origin, but Gunflint historian Sue Kerfoot, said that the "Gunflint Trail" label began appearing in the local newspaper early in the 1920s.

During this time, the Trail remained a narrow, brushy and rocky passageway until 1924 when the county, newly aware of the tourist potential of their glorious avenue through the Superior National Forest, constructed a real road over the path of Henry Mayhew's wagon road from Grand Marais to Gunflint Lake. It wasn't until the late 1930s, when the Civilian Conservation Corps built the last 20 miles of road from the Cross River Bridge to Seagull Lake, that the Gunflint Trail became the only north/south road to bisect the county.

Several years later, two resort operators on Lake Saganaga, Russell Blankenburg and Art Nunsted, built the last mile to the water border as a private road and charged a toll so that their guests had to pay a dollar to get to their resorts. Blankenburg and Nunsted eventually sold their road to the county, but it wasn't until 1953 that this segment was irrigated and surfaced to complete the 56-mile Gunflint Trail that took 62 years to build.

The Gunflint Trail has had many configurations over the last hundred years because of changing traveler destinations, shifting county political agendas and the technology of road building equipment. There are several segments of the old Trail or braids of others, now county roads, forest roads or foot trails that are fascinating to follow.

One of the usable, remaining segments of the original Gunflint Trail is the nine-mile stretch of gravel County Highway 92—the Iron Lake Road—that turns off the Trail at the north end of Poplar Lake and follows a roller coaster ride over ridges and through swamps. An interesting remnant of the old days on this road is the old Gunflint Post Office near Iron Lake gussied up now as a private home, but which served for many years in the days when The Gunflint Tail was considered a discrete mailing address.

The Gunflint Trail, from its beginning at the corner of Highway 61 and Highway 12 in Grand Marais to its watery conclusion at the End of the Trail Campground, is a storied landscape of courage, incredible labor, failure and frustration, exploitation and abandonment, discovery and renewal. Left alone virtually without population or habitation for almost a half century and allowed to mature by itself, The Trail ripened to great natural beauty and to the magic of wild places.

Norton & Peel, Minnesota Historical Society

One of the most beautiful lakes in Minnesota, Seagull was featured for many years in the Land of Sky Blue Waters print advertising and movies for the Hamm Brewing Company of St. Paul.

Perhaps one of the reasons, other than its great natural beauty, many are fascinated by the Gunflint Trail, is that in many ways it is an echo of yesterday. Other than the road width and surface, The Trail really hasn't changed much in the past century. There aren't many permanent residents (approximately 200) and very few houses along it.

The signature, or trademark of the Gunflint Trail, is a grove of about fifty majestic white pines the Trail bisects seven miles up from Grand Marais. Most of these trees are between 300 and 350 years old and are the only living witnesses to the entire history of the Gunflint Trail. Originally they were part of the Weyerhauser Lumber Company's holdings which included about five townships of white pine extending south to Elbow Lake, but are now part of the Superior National Forest. The area was all logged except for this grove, yet no one knows why these trees were spared. Wes Hedstrom, who has planted many white and red pines in this area since 1950, says almost all these remaining pines are rotten inside and will probably begin falling down sometime in the near future. Anna Johnson, a founder of the Grand Marais art culture, memorialized the Gunflint Pines almost a century ago in an oil painting that still hangs in the Johnson Heritage Post in downtown Grand Marais.

Cameron Norman

The view from the overlook on Pincushion Mountain at the south end of the Gunflint Trail takes in the city of Grand Marais, (Great Harbor in Old French), the Sawtooth mountains marching down the shore, and a 100-mile-expanse of Lake Superior.

From the top of Pincushion Mountain, the view toward town and the Big Lake is the last the visitor will have of the more familiar world. From there north, the Gunflint is the "long shadowed forest," hiking trails, pristine water, secluded cabins and resorts, canoe outfitters, moose crossings, undulating northern lights and silence.

The Gunflint Trail area is not about commerce. It has no shopping malls, golf courses or swimming pools, no fast food restaurants, trailer parks, nightclubs, cineplexes, billboards or developments. It is approximately 70 percent forest, 25 percent lakes and rivers, 5 percent dwellings and roads. It has some resorts, B & Bs, canoe outfitters, cabins and guide services, but nothing that could be called a business community. The natural beauty of folded terrain, majestic forest and clean water has been kept almost unaltered for 100 years.

Gunflint Lodge

Gunflint Lake is nine miles long, a mile wide and lies along an east/west line giving the prevailing westerlies a clean sweep down the lake, often piling up great breakers in the open water. Here a canoeist enjoys an infrequent serene moment on this often tumultuous lake.

The Lake: Jewel of The Gunflint

Gunflint is a bluish-gray, slightly opaque silicate mineral, that shows pepper flakes when held to the light. It is often found in conjunction with the rocks that held Gunflint iron. For a time, early in the 19th century, the lake appeared on some maps as Redground Lake "from the ochery red gravel that abounds." Later, after David Thompson surveyed and mapped the area, it was known as Flinty Lake on English maps, but since 1850 it has been called Gunflint.

Through the glory days of the fur trade, a steady stream of laden canoes passed through Gunflint Lake on the Voyageur's Highway. LaVerendrye, Sir Alexander Mackenzie, Peter Pond, Daniel Harmon, Sir George Simpson, David

Thompson, all the giants of the Fur Century passed this way, bringing their flotillas of trade and exploration.

The eight-mile-long Gunflint Lake is unique on the Voyageur's Highway as it is one of the larger lakes in the border chain, and a major destination and passage during the Fur Century, but is not in the Boundary Waters Canoe Area Wilderness. Perhaps the mining activity, the railroad, heavy private investments, political clout and resort development kept the area from wilderness designation. Today there are about one hundred private properties on Gunflint Lake. The remaining shoreline on the American side is owned by the federal government and managed by the U.S. Forest Service, while the Canadian side is mostly Crown land, with a few sections in private ownership.

During the 1890s, when logging and mining brought so much activity and a growing population to Gunflint Lake, there was even a steamer, the Zena, carrying freight and passengers on a daily schedule. But there has been no commercial activity on the lake for decades, with the exception of some liquor smuggling from Canada into Minnesota during the years of Prohibition. One stormy night, back in the 30s, a boatload of illegal rye whiskey went to the bottom and, although some enterprising scuba divers have tried repeatedly to locate the wreck, it has never been found.

Also during the 1890s, while Henry Mayhew was locating and testing his iron mines at the west end of the lake, another man came into the country. He was a more solitary, reclusive man who left a legacy of luostari—the beautiful Finnish word meaning sanctuary, or cloister—that would put an unintended stamp on the Gunflint region. His name was George Wartner, and no one knows exactly who he was or where he came from. Today, he is little more than a vague footnote in regional histories. What we do know is that he arrived in the area about 1891 and built a cabin on what is now known as Wartner's Bay on the north shore of Gunflint Lake. He spent most of his time trapping, gardening and hunting, although he did occasionally walk or snowshoe to Grand Marais and back to Gunflint a couple times a year.

In the green, black and gray diorama of the Gunflint forest it is hard to visualize a multi-colored, floral extravaganza ever existing here. But there was such a spot: it was George Wartner's garden. Apparently, he was a feisty old guy, cantankerous as a hungry bear, forever scrapping with game wardens, county commissioners and his neighbors. But for all his grumbling, Wartner had an abiding love of wilderness and flowers.

After clearing the forest from around his cabin, he planted an arboretum of pansies, sweet Williams, lilacs, roses, juneberries and a wide variety of trees and shrubs. What a contrast that must have been! There in the middle of the somber forest was an Eden of color, a luxuriant blanket of flowering plants covering the rocky ground. Buried somewhere under that blustery Wartner exterior was a poet's soul.

The years passed and one winter day old George Wartner drowned near Camper's Island in a suspicious accident. The cabin burned down and the forest gradually reclaimed much of the site, but the flowers and shrubs continued to bloom for many years. Occasionally, residents or cabin owners would pull their boats quietly into Wartner's Bay, dig out a few plants and hurry back to replant them on their property.

Today many properties on Gunflint Lake have Wartner cherry trees, lilac bushes or a clump of sweet Williams blooming in their yards. The big lilac bush at the southwest corner of Gunflint Lodge came originally from George Wartner's garden. These are tributes to the feisty old pioneer who brought a colorful palette with him to the wilderness.

From Gunflint Lake, many canoeists paddle to Lake Superior through the border lakes, the Pigeon River and over the nine mile Grand Portage. Frequent, idyllic rest stops like this along the way make it a pleasant trip.

Justine Kerfoot arrived for a visit at Gunflint Lodge in 1926 as a Northwestern University student to help her mother with their new resort. She fell in love with the area and never left.

CHAPTER 3

Gunflint Characters: Builders of the Name

There is something sinewy, strong-minded and a little eccentric about country builders and it has much to do with the ruggedness and remoteness of the land they shape. John Madson defines this well in *Where the Sky Began*, when he says, "Regional character is a reflection of the land."

Another approach to this relationship between personalities and landscape is found in William Horwath's introduction to John McPhee's *Pine Barrens*. He writes about the natives of that wild, lonely part of New Jersey, a region he calls both an archetype and another country: "These people are usually so at variance with modern norms that they become perfect descendants of America's original stock, single-minded pursuers of freedom and independence, fiercely self reliant."

The Gunflint country was opened by men of vision and incredible energy—Henry Mayhew, Sam Howenstine, Ted Wakelin and many others—men who pioneered and persevered, but with a shrewd eye to economic gain. Some succeeded, some didn't, but their memories now seem the dusty stuff of local history. Perhaps there is a road or lake named for them, or maybe there is an historic site plaque that commemorates their homestead, but it was mostly the men and women who came later without a political or economic agenda who have focused most attention on the Gunflint region.

Over the century there have been many of these whose often vinegary personalities would define this land: strong, unconventional, independent men and women who never really fit into any of the niches other segments of their society offered. The Bird Lady of the Trail, Molly Hoffman, sums it up: "Even today," she says, "there is less homogeneity on The Trail, so to be different is to fit."

Drawn inexorably to beautiful, sparsely populated country, their strange lifestyles, heroic deeds and unique value systems have added vivid and varied colors to the Gunflint tapestry.

Ben Gallagher

"It's a poor rich family that can't afford at least one playboy," was Ben Gallagher's response when anyone questioned his lifestyle.

This northern forest has seldom been the habitat of playboys, so Ben was something of a curiosity here. Unemployed by choice, but independently wealthy, Ben was a trap and skeet shooting champion, world traveler, and owner of a picture book chalet on a Minnesota wilderness island, a Montana cattle ranch and a chateau in France. Ben Gallagher was a character straight from an F. Scott Fitzgerald novel and a Gunflint legend. What set him apart from his neighbors was not just his wealth and lifestyle, but also his independent spirit and his occasional outrageous behavior.

Today when canoeists pass through Magnetic Lake on their way to Little Rock Falls, the Granite River and out into Saganaga, they have to pass Ben Gallagher's Island near the northwest shore. Most ship their paddles and pause for a moment in surprise and wonder at the island with its beautiful home, guest cabins, colorful gardens and manicured lawn, all maintained in Gallagher fashion by the present owner. It is somewhat jarring and incongruous in its wilderness setting, but then, so was Ben Gallagher.

Ben was born in Omaha, scion of a wealthy Nebraska merchant family whose business history went back to the Oregon and Mormon Trails along the Platte River. They had a wholesale grocery that provisioned pioneer wagon trains. Through astute management and vision (although not Ben's) the company prospered and expanded over the years and still operates successfully today. It is unclear whether Ben ever worked a day in the family business because he spent most of his summers on the island in Magnetic Lake and winters at his chateau in France.

His first cabin was on the western shore of Gunflint Lake, but it burned and in 1928 he bought the island in Magnetic Bay from Oden Wick and began the gingerbread enclave on the two-thirds acre outcrop of granite that was to become Gallagher's Island. His pet beaver Sam is memorialized in oak atop the newel post of the main cabin stairway. Sam figures in many of the Ben Gallagher stories and one, in particular, seems to survive.

Ben had notified his chauffeur that he had to make a "business" trip to Duluth and that he should pack the car (the only Rolls Royce the Gunflint had ever seen), and cautioned him not to forget Sam, who traveled in a crate in the trunk of the car. They arrived in Duluth late in the afternoon and after Ben and Sam had checked into their room in the Duluth Hotel, Ben filled the bathtub so Sam could have a little play area.

In the early evening Ben went down to the dining room and later stopped at the Black Bear Lounge for a relaxing drink or two. It was quite late when he got back to the room, which was in shambles.

Apparently Sam had gotten bored with the bathtub, climbed out and went exploring. He began to sample the base-boards, chair legs, a walnut armoire, the bedstead and several other pieces of furniture. The room damage cost Ben about $4,000, not a lot today, perhaps, but a princely sum in the middle of the Great Depression.

Ben was used to buying his way out of sticky situations, and the habit followed him to the grave. His will provided instructions for a very large sum of money to be made available to the church "for a series of masses for the repose of my soul."

One old time resident recalls that before Ben met his wife, Lucille, and settled down, Ben had a number of lady friends, some of whom shared the island delights with him. Ben had bought an upright piano from a Duluth music store for one of his companions and came up with a unique plan to get it out to the island. From Duluth to Loon Lake was a relatively easy trucking job, but road problems beyond Loon Lake necessitated the piano be rafted across Loon Lake to the Gunflint Portage and hauled on poles across the two-mile portage by some of Ben's Native American employees. Then the raft was re-built and the piano floated across Gunflint and Magnetic to the island.

The memories of old neighbors are sometimes a little faulty, but there is general agreement that although she liked the piano, Lucille felt uncomfortable with its colorful history and decided she no longer wanted the piano on the island. Resort owner Justine Kerfoot agreed to take it over to Gunflint Lodge, so she towed two canoes (lashed together to form a pontoon float for the piano) behind a power boat over to the island. Off the piano went on its back across the lake to Gunflint Lodge where it was enjoyed for many years until it became another casualty of the June, 1953 fire that burned the lodge to the ground.

Benny Ambrose

The Gunflint had another Ben. Benjamin Quentin Ambrose, of Ottertrack Lake, born on an Iowa farm in 1896 (as best he could recollect). He came to the Gunflint region around 1920, worked some at logging and mineral prospecting with Russell Blankenburg. Like most prospectors he had many stories about "lost gold mines" and great deposits of silver, nickel and asbestos, but he made his living primarily by trapping and guiding. Former U.S. Navy Secretary, James Forrestal claimed Benny was the best guide he had ever fished with.

He was the only man ever given lifetime tenancy when the Boundary Waters Canoe Area Wilderness was taken over by the U.S. Government and all private property was eliminated. His cabin, which never got completely built, was on a beautiful point of Ottertrack Lake (called Cypress Lake on newer maps), west of the Monument Portage from Saganaga.

He acquired the land and started his cabin in 1929, but somehow he never got around to completing it. In 1937 he married Val McIlhenny, who was resorter Justine Kerfoot's college roommate at Northwestern University and who worked during the summer at Gunflint Lodge. They had two daughters: Bonnie, who was born at the cabin in 1940, and Holly, born in the Grand Marais hospital in 1946. In a biographical essay on the life of Benny Ambrose in *Minnesota History* magazine, Ralph Wright-Peterson sketched the bumpy course of this unusual marriage.

"Bonnie, their first daughter later recalled: 'Mother got through those winters somehow. I don't know how, but she did. There was no cabin until later—much later. She used to sleep with potatoes in her sleeping bag to keep them from freezing.' Bonnie also remembered that when they baked bread on top of the stove in the winter, part of the loaf would bake and the rest would freeze."

Later Holly wrote, "We had everything kids could want: freedom and what seemed like the whole world to spend it in....There were no other kids, but we didn't notice. For pets we had a dog named Fritz, snakes, raccoons and some-times wolf pups if Dad happened to trap them, birds, squirrels, otter, martens—you name it we had it, but not in cages though."

The family shared the rugged wilderness life for ten years, but after Holly was born, Val insisted on moving to civilization so their daughters could go to school and have playmates. Ben refused to give up his home and Val left, taking the girls with her. In 1951 the couple divorced without bitterness, each under-standing the other's needs.

Benny continued to expand his large vegetable and flower garden, which Val had encouraged him to start. It eventually grew to truck farm proportions, growing produce he shared with everyone, particularly canoe trippers who would stop on the point for a visit. There were always carrots, onions, rutabagas, potatoes, radishes, lettuce and a wide variety of fruit from his orchard. This was rocky infertile country, but Ben used to gather the decomposing organic material from around beaver lodges and haul bags of it in his canoe and over portages to spread on his expanding vegetable garden. Also, whenever he went back to Iowa for a visit, he would take large bags and boxes to fill with rich, black soil.

Benny was a lithe, wiry welterweight, about 5' 10", 165 pounds, and used to paddle, portage and walk the 70 miles to Grand Marais to play shortstop on the local baseball team, to attend parties or to vote. He claimed to have never missed an election and to always be the first one in line when the polls opened in the morning.

Another of his notable physical feats was running down fishers, the large, dark brown musteline relative of the pine marten and the weasel, which he would catch alive and sell to fur farm owners in Two Harbors, who would pay up to $100 per animal for use as breeding stock. It might take him three days to catch the fisher, but he never gave up and eventually cornered the exhausted animal and stuffed him in his sack.

Benny had a heart attack at 80 while trapping beaver at Pettigony Lake while up to his waist in water. He got out of the lake, drove his tractor to the house of a friend who had a plane and who flew him to Grand Marais for a 19 day hospital stay.

One early September day in 1982, a U.S. Forest Service plane on fire patrol flew over the cabin as the pilot usually did each day to check on the 86-year-old hermit and spotted the burned out remains of the outdoor kitchen and Benny's body lying near it. It was surmised that the kitchen caught fire and in the exertion of trying to put it out, Benny suffered a fatal heart attack.

There are commemorative markers along the rock ledges of Ottertrack (Cypress) Lake on both sides of the border with metal etchings of Benny in his trademark open-throated plaid shirt and shapeless black hat, the date of his death and a question mark after the1896 birth date.

Columnist Ron Seely wrote in *Canoe* magazine: "In time the point will again be as Ambrose found it, and the old man will be but a memory, growing fainter with time, just as the laughter of the loon fades almost imperceptibly into silence when dusk turns into night in the North Country."

There were many other of these eccentric characters along the Gunflint Corridor for nearly a century. Most of the men seemed to have similar agendas: to get into wild country away from cities and social strictures, to hunt, fish and trap, to reject authority and to be as self-reliant as possible.

Women of the Gunflint

The Gunflint women stand out splendidly and in boldest relief. They were prodigious workers, compassionate, capable and tough as saddle leather. They acted as midwives, cleared the land, built cabins and resorts, operated heavy road-building equipment, guided sportsmen, installed plumbing and strung telephone wire through the wilderness.

They were trappers, dog mushers and loggers. They cut and stored ice for summer refrigeration and cut wood for winter heat. Then they changed hats and became hostesses, business managers, writers, community leaders, wives and mothers—strong, resourceful women, unafraid of wild country and its challenges.

There was a precedent for these women here. Across Gunflint Lake on the Canadian side, near the Magnetic Narrows, is the site of an old Native American village. The women of Cree and Ojibwe blood who inhabited this village as late as the mid-1900s provided role models for those white women who came into the Gunflint country. From what we know of that village and those women, it was a matriarchal society with women like Mary Netowance, Mrs. Cook, Mrs. Spoon, Mrs. Plummer, Ahbutch, Mrs. Spruce and Mrs. Tamarack, the most memorable members. They taught their new neighbors how to hunt and fish, to trap beaver, to survive the extremes of weather, to use native plants for medicines, to make moccasins and snowshoes, and to cure and tan hides. Most importantly perhaps, they taught them to live by nature's calendar, to observe and learn in nature's classroom.

This concept of Native American women mentoring and serving as role models for their white neighbors is corroborated in Victoria Brehm's *Women's Great Lakes Reader.* In the introduction she says:

"North American Indian women owned the property they created, such as their lodges, they controlled the maple sugaring and ricing lands, they had the power of voting on important community decisions, and they could divorce their husbands and retain custody of the children...power white women did not receive until the twentieth century. Native women's independent self sufficiency was a strong example."

In her master's thesis entitled *Women of the Gunflint Trail*, Catherine R. Peterson categorized Gunflint women by their residency dates:

Pre-1900: Women established homes and businesses with absentee partners (husbands were hunting or trapping most of the time) - these were women of pioneer spirit and strength who daily dealt with survival for themselves and their families.

1900-1929: Women and men were co-workers and business partners.

1930-1949: A depressed nation followed by a world war sent women to the Gunflint region in search of jobs.

1950-1969: Women with formal educational backgrounds started arriving. This group of women shared a love of nature, a need for peace and quiet and a healthy respect for individuality. They may also have been running away from the hectic pace and turmoil of the times. An education is never lost and each of these women has enriched The Trail with their varied backgrounds, education, expertise and experience.

Eve Blankenburg

The Gunflint women were of a little different stripe than the men, more ambitious and creative. Perhaps because they had to be. On Seagull Lake there was Eve Blankenburg, the scrupulously thrifty road builder, resorter, shrewd investor and ultimate recycler. Each spring, Eve used to go down to Gunflint Lodge to collect the big corrugated cardboard cartons the new outboard motors came in, flatten them out and insulate, or "wallpaper," their one-room, 12' by 14' cabin. She also took the coffee grounds, shrimp tails and old lettuce leaves from the lodge kitchen to her composting pile for her vegetable garden on Seagull Creek.

One day, driving down the Gunflint Trail, I saw Eve leaning up against a jack pine at the Extortion Lake corner looking like she just stepped off the ramp at a style show. She was absolutely elegant in an obviously expensive burgundy silk suit. She had been at a friend's wedding reception at their Extortion Lake cabin and was hitchhiking back to Seagull. But my lasting image of Eve, who died recently at 92, will always be of her sitting on a big, yellow D9 Cat bulldozer, guiding it over her new road, tree trunks and rocks scattered higgledy-piggledy on either side, with the controls in one hand and the *Wall Street Journal* in the other. Her neighbor and friend, Ardis David, said at Eve's memorial service, "She was the most unique, surprising, delightful individual I have ever met."

Katy Lush

Katy Lush, or Dr. Catherine Burns, as she is known professionally, never formally established a medical practice in Cook County, but for years was the only physician and first medical responder in the Gunflint Tail area to attend to all the axe cuts, heart attacks, campfire burns, allergy reactions, chain saw wounds, broken bones, appendicitis attacks and other emergencies that demanded immediate attention. She never hung out a shingle and never solicited or charged for medical services, but felt ethically bound to help when she was needed.

Katy began showing the Gunflint Woman qualities of strength and independence early on. She graduated from the University of Minnesota Medical School in 1938, when a University rule stated that only ten percent of a medical class could be women. An early flying enthusiast, she obtained her pilot's license in 1939. With her family and her helpful neighbors she built her first cabin on Gunflint Lake in 1940. Katy loved the area and spent as much of her time as possible at the cabin, although her medical practice was in Albert Lea, Duluth and later in Minneapolis.

One day in the late '40s, a Seagull Lake neighbor, 15-year-old Everett Watters, was splitting firewood and accidentally cut his arm badly with the axe. His uncle Frances, a bush pilot who lived nearby, wrapped Ev's arm in a blanket, got him into the plane and took off for Grand Marais where there was medical help at the tiny Cook County Hospital. When they arrived at the Devil Track Airport, Frances discovered that neither the one physician nor his nurse were in town that day, so he radioed back to see if Katy was at Gunflint. Fortunately, she was. Frances headed back and landed the floatplane at Katy's dock, but by that time the makeshift bandage had come loose, the plane's cabin was blood-spattered and the patient was in danger of going into deep shock. Katy's initial treatment was started in the plane's cabin and then Everett was carried inside by Frances and Katy's husband Cliff, where she completed the job of sewing up tendons, veins, muscles and skin. Everett recovered completely. In telling the story, Katy says that in all the wounds she has treated in this region, no infections have ever resulted. "I guess we don't have any bugs up here," she says.

Peggy Heston

In spite of all the obstacles and lack of medical care, these Gunflint women were remarkably rugged and their longevity is legendary. Peggy Heston retired at 90 from her job as guide and hostess at the Johnson Heritage Post in Grand Marais. She always walked the eight blocks back and forth to work from her apartment in year-round weather, found time for a little cross country skiing in the winter and still enjoys reminiscing about her 40 years on Gunflint Lake as the tiny dynamo and co-founder of Heston's Lodge. She bought her first pair of cross country skis at age 60 and taught herself how to use them on the snow-covered lake early in the morning after preparing hearty guest breakfasts of sourdough pancakes and eggs. "I would get out on the lake by 7:00 a.m.," she told writer Anna Klobuchar recently. "I still remember those mornings, being out there, completely alone and surround by complete peace. Oh, those mornings were just beautiful."

Alis Brandt

The matriarch of the Gunflint was Alis Brandt, who died a few days short of 105. She and her husband Carl built Nor'Wester Lodge on Poplar Lake in 1931. Her obituary in the Cook County News Herald noted that, like most resort partners, she had a killer work schedule: cooking, baking, cutting firewood, skinning beavers, picking berries, baking pies and a couple dozen loaves of bread a day, packing the ice house, pumping gas, and doing all the laundry. The Herald made a special note of that process: "Her laundry system involved four tubs in a circle with the washing machine in the center which swung the wringer around to all four tubs. She carried the water by hand from the lake, split the wood and heated the water in a barrel. She could do up to a hundred sheets at a time"...then "she did her toning exercises to keep up her strength and muscle tone." At 97 she "retired" from baking 16 loaves of the famous Nor'Wester bread a day and picking blueberries for the pies.

It helps to have the Methuselah gene, but there seems to be something else at work here. Dr. Bernie Siegal wrote: "It is interesting that in the United States, the states with the largest numbers of people over 85 are Maine, North Dakota and Minnesota. (And nearly 70 percent of them are women.) The point I make is that these are states where the living conditions have not been the easiest, and I think that people from these areas learn to be survivors from the beginning. They are independent, willing to take on life, and are used to providing for themselves."

Dinna Madsen

A woman whose fame has spread beyond the Gunflint region is Dinna Madsen. Her given name is Virginia, but Dinna is a sibling's childhood interpretation of "dynamite," and so she has been for 81 years. She and her late husband, Art, a Canadian ranger, trapper and guide, operated Camp Saganto on the 460-acre Red Pine Island on the Canadian side of Saganaga since 1946.

In Anna Klobuchar's feature on Dinna in the Cook County News Herald, she reveals the tender but tough side of this typical Gunflint woman: "The kids felt there was nothing Mom couldn't do. She stitched up an injured duckling using red thread and a baseball stitch, after sterilizing the needle and tucking the duckling's stomach back into its body cavity. It survived. She shot and killed an injured bear which had swung loose from a trap and was attacking a neighbor."

Some of Dinna's six pregnancies outdo the stories of pioneer women walking West who, according to legend, stopped in a shady spot, had their baby and got back in line. Dinna says, "If you had to write the life story of my early years, you could call it, 'Struggling and Pregnant.'" Klobuchar tells the story of the Snowshoe Baby, a story that was picked up by Associated Press and printed internationally:

"One of Dinna's well known stories took place in the brutal winter of 1956. In January of that year, Dinna, at the end of her ninth month of pregnancy, needed to get to the nearest hospital, which was in Duluth, to have the baby. On the way out from the island, the propeller-driven snow machine broke down, and Dinna, with son Chris in tow, had to snowshoe across the frozen lake and the adjoining wilderness, stopping once to make a fire in the -20 degree weather. As the baby kicked and stirred, Dinna and Chris made their way to the landing at the top of the Gunflint, where Dinna caught a ride in a snowplow, then a bus, to Duluth. Helen Sue was born there, cozy and safe. To this day she is Madsen's 'snowshoe baby.'"

The image for the ultimate tough yet tender Gunflint Woman was undoubtedly Shawbogeeziboh, daughter of Chief Blackstone who, according to author Shirley Peruniak in *Quetico Provincial Park*, reports Shirley Powell as saying that they had found a tiny, orphaned cub bear and gave it to Shawbogeeziboh who "was breast feeding one of her babies, so she fed the baby out of one of her breasts and the baby bear out of the other."

Nature writer, Helen Hoover, whose books about life in the forest and their primitive cabin on Gunflint Lake sold in the millions, focused the nation's attention on the Gunflint region in the1960s and '70s. She and her artist husband, Ade, came to the Gunflint from Chicago in 1954 to live and work totally immersed in the wilderness experience in a one-room log cabin with no amenities: no car (after a wreck on the Trail), no running water, electricity or plumbing and often, very little food. But Helen survived because she was an intensely resolute woman, a trait she shared with most Gunflint women of her time.

There were many of these unconventional women, whose vigorous personalities added a robust earthiness to the Gunflint region. Four of them were neighbors and seemed to have an extra dash of the Gunflint style.

Tempest Powell

The heritage of this country is as much Native American as it is French/Canadian or American settler. There were Ojibwe in the Gunflint region, Cree to the north, Algonquin to the east, Assiniboin and Sioux to the west. There was never a large Native American population in Cook County— mostly small villages, scattered cabins and eventually a reservation—but it was the Native Americans' country until 1854 when the Treaty of La Pointe allowed white settlement.

In spite of sometimes clashing cultures, there were also some intermarriages such as that between the English/Irish Jack Powell, a logger working in the Ely area, and Mary Ottertail, of the Lac La Croix band of Ojibwe. They had five children, the youngest of whom was Tempest, who became the prototype Gunflint woman because she stood with a foot in both worlds and was the connection between the modern Gunflint woman and the cultural folkways that would define the region.

Tempest was born on the Powell "farm" on Ontario's Lake Saganagons, 18 canoe miles and a long portage from the end of the Gunflint Trail, where Native American spirituality, natural medicines, wilderness skills, respect and love of family were dispensed in equal measure, primarily by Mary Ottertrack. Jack's task was to teach the children to read and write as there were no schools anywhere nearby. It was traditional in Native American families not to name a child immediately at birth but rather wait for a dream, an event or some natural association to suggest a name. After witnessing one of her temper tantrums at a family gathering, Jack decided Tempest would be a fitting name.

There are hundreds of Tempest Powell stories still circulating in the Gunflint region. There was Tempest the beaver trapper and dog team musher separating eight snapping dogs and a furious mother bear. Tempest the beautiful fishing guide, quickly and effectively handling amorous fishermen. Tempest the forest fire fighter, staying on the fire line until everyone else was out. But the one story that portrays Tempest at her best was told by Justine Kerfoot.

In the 1920s and 30s there was no mail delivery up the Trail, so everyone who lived up there had everything sent to Gunflint Lodge, where they then picked up their mail. They had a Sears Roebuck catalogue at the little store at the lodge and most residents did their Christmas shopping from it.

Tempest had three little daughters and she had ordered dolls for them, but delivery was late, so two days before Christmas, Tempest hitched up her dog team and took off for Gunflint Lodge in a blizzard. For a day and part of the night she mushed across Saganaga, down the Granite River, across the lakes, over the winter portages and through the forest to the Lodge. She picked up her packages but time was getting short, so she turned her team around and started back without any rest or food, arriving just in time for Christmas.

Clara Dewar

Loon Lake Clara, who came here from Fergus Falls about 90 years ago, was short but probably the physically strongest woman in the area. Willard Johnson, a later owner of Loon Lake Lodge, tells stories of Clara literally building some of the resort buildings alone and by hand. She found the pines she wanted for cabin logs on a ridge across the lake, had them felled, limbed and rafted across the lake in the summer or skidded them across the ice in the winter, and built the cabins and lodge with not much more than muscle and a few elementary tools.

She had a husband and he helped some, but he was a restless entrepreneur-type who preferred to buy faltering businesses, build them up and sell them. At one time or another, he had a logging company in Canada, a bar in Two Harbors, an automobile dealership in Michigan's Upper Peninsula and several other enterprises, some of them all going at once. He would stay around and guide fishermen or work on the cabins for a while, but then drift off to another business adventure for several months. Clara preferred to stay at Loon Lake and build. Willard recalls seeing her sitting on top of the cabin ridgepole, swinging her hammer and singing at the top of her lungs.

To many local residents during the Depression years, beaver trapping was a tempting way to supplement meager budgets. Having a legal season for this activity was sometimes an inconvenience but never an obstacle for many locals. Clara, who was one of the best beaver trappers, always seemed to have a cash flow problem, so a bundle of prime beaver hides was often the answer to her sticky financial problems.

One early winter day before the beaver trapping season opened, Clara snowshoed out to check her traps along a line she had established in the bush and bog country west of Iron Lake when a sudden whiteout snowstorm enveloped her. She lost her bearings, and stumbled around for a while trying to locate some familiar landmarks, but soon realized she was lost and was going to have to spend the night in the woods. By this time, she had enough beaver hides to fill her big Duluth pack, so she stuffed them and herself into a rot-hollowed pine log for the night hoping the weather would clear by morning.

In those days, folks never went into the woods alone without letting someone know where and when they were going and when they expected to return. A neighbor knew Clara was overdue and alerted other neighbors, the U.S. Forest Service Seagull Guard station and the game wardens.

As is still the case in this neighborhood, when someone is in trouble, the entire available population turns out to help. By morning, there were a couple dozen people on the Iron Lake Road fully equipped for a search along Clara's trap line. They went through the woods practically arm in arm until they found her: cold, hungry and cramped up from her night in the hollow log, but otherwise feisty as ever and able to snowshoe back to the road.

Clara and the rescue party got back to Loon Lake Lodge early in the afternoon—too early to go home and too late to go back to work— so they decided to have a Welcome Home Clara party that went on into the night. There was an adequate supply of food and bourbon in the lodge so it was a convivial group, many of whom returned the next day to retrieve choppers, snowshoes, packsacks and other items forgotten in the fellowship of the evening.

Another forgotten item, at least by the game wardens, was the Duluth pack full of illegal beaver hides. One of the wardens guessed later that they were all so glad to have Clara back safely, they clean forgot about those beaver hides.

Mamma Gallagher

Mamma (Lucille) Gallagher was another of those Gunflint women who combined an iron will with care and compassion, but always with a Gallic flair.

She was born in LePecq, France, a village near Paris, and met her husband Ben Gallagher under unusual circumstances. He was a member of an American trap and skeet shooting team competing in France. Mamma, also a crack wingshot, was a member of the French women's team and they met at the tournament. They were married shortly after and Ben brought Mamma and their Belgian servants, Artur and Yvonne, back to Gunflint. Imagine the culture shock: from gay Paris to a wilderness island on the Canadian border!

Strangely, the name Lucille seems to have gotten lost when people recollect Mamma Gallagher. In the memories, letters and feature articles from friends and residents, anywhere her name was used it was almost always "Mamma Gallagher." Justine Kerfoot told me the name was given to her early because of her constant attention to everyone's welfare. She always saw to it that the children in the Native American village across the lake had warm winter clothes and boots. No one went hungry when Mamma was around. Christmas presents were always lavishly distributed and hard luck stories always got a sympathetic ear from Mamma Gallagher. She must have eventually considered Gunflint home because she lived at Heston's in the cabin on the point for 13 years after Ben died in 1966.

Old-timers here have their own favorite Mamma or Ben story, but the one old Lucas likes to tell concerns the time Mamma decided Ben could use a little more culture. She hired a French tutor for Ben, who held daily language sessions in a room above the boathouse. Things seemed to be going well until Mamma noticed Ben's accomplishment level dropping precipitously. She slipped over to the boathouse one day to see if she could determine the reason for Ben's backsliding and discovered the lesson for that day involved Ben teaching the tutor to drink sour mash bourbon. The tutor was disciplined and Ben went on indefinite probation.

A close friend and neighbor of Justine Kerfoot at Gunflint Lodge, Mamma was disapproving and quite vocal about Justine's usual garb of rubber-bottomed boots, wool trousers, plaid shirt and a shapeless old guide's hat—a costume that would get her in trouble more than once. Mamma felt that as a resort owner with a growing clientele of upscale customers, Justine should, at least sometimes, be more elegantly dressed.

Like many convent-raised French girls, Mamma was an excellent seamstress, and soon set about making Justine a blue silk dress, which she felt would be appropriate for her hostess duties. She had made the former room above the boathouse—where Ben and his tutor got into so much trouble—into a light, airy sewing room and spent hours on the intricate detailing of Justine's new dress. When she presented the dress to Justine at the annual Christmas party Gunflint Lodge always gave for the neighbors, Mrs. Spruce and Mrs. Tamarack remarked that it was the most beautiful dress they had ever seen.

Many years later, when Justine was relating the story to me, I asked: "Whatever happened to that dress?"

"I don't know," she harrumphed. "I never wore the damn thing."

Justine Kerfoot

Justine was a Gunflint Trail icon for over 70 years. Her mailbox just said "Justine." There was never any need for more identification because there was no other Justine. Our Lady of the Trail.

Justine Spunner Kerfoot came to Gunflint Lake from Illinois in 1927 when her mother bought Gunflint Lodge from Russell Blankenburg. She was a Northwestern University medical student at the time and she came to the resort one summer vacation to help her mother out and was so enthralled with the Gunflint country that she never left.

Perhaps because she lived in the Gunflint region longer than anyone and was, for all those years, one of the most colorful residents, there are more Justine stories than bear stories. Many of them have Justine's wardrobe as their subject.

She never was a slave to fashion and never really made the apparel transition from fishing guide to resort hostess and celebrity, even though she made many public appearances before Congressional committees, and at book signings and lectures. Most of the time, around the resort she preferred her fishing guide apparel. Indeed, that is how she is dressed in the large oil portrait over the entrance to the main dining room in Gunflint Lodge.

Justine never lost her fascination with, and her need-to-know attitude about, wild places. One of her favorite pastimes was to drive her car anywhere there was a hint of a road with her friend and neighbor, Charlotte Merrick, through the woods, over rocks, hubcap deep in the swamps or through the aspen and raspberry thickets of the clearcut hills. "Just lookin' around," Justine would say.

One of the early problems was that this fascination was a little much for her standard model station wagon and when she got stuck, she'd hike out and call the lodge for someone to come and pick her up. Naturally, when four-wheel drive SUV's became popular, Justine had to have one.

One July day she decided she would try to get through the Cross River ski trail that paralleled the river several miles from the lodge. It had been a wet year and the land adjacent to river was shifty and water-logged. She hadn't gone far in that muck before she was sinking rapidly, all four wheels spinning and the frame hopelessly hung up on the saturated ground.

She decided to bushwhack out through the woods to the Gunflint Trail and hitch hike back to the lodge or to a phone. Mud-spattered, her usual work pants and plaid shirt dirty, disheveled and torn, she stood there for half an hour waving her thumb as the cars whizzed past, pretending not to see her.

At that time Justine Kerfoot was probably one of the best known women in Minnesota. She was the subject of many newspaper articles, magazine features, television specials and was much in demand as a speaker and at book signings. Had the people in the passing cars realized that that ragged-looking figure at the side of the road was Justine Kerfoot, they would have been thrilled to give her a ride. A resident finally came along in his old pickup, knew immediately who it was, and took her back to Gunflint Lodge.

Mamma Gallagher said, "Justine, I told you something like that would happen!"

Often obscured by the humor and color of the typical Justine story is her unyielding will and curiosity about people, places and how things work. She tackled a job like establishing the first telephone service on The Trail without having any idea how to go about it. She strung the wires on trees, attached the equipment and kept trying it out. If it didn't work, she'd determine why it didn't work, start all over again and eventually get it working. One month she would be deep in the innards of a big pump's engine or the lodge plumbing system, or assisting in the birth of a Native American child across the lake. The next month she'd be in the Easter Islands, trying to puzzle out the origin of stone monoliths. The very next she would be in Washington, D.C., testifying before a Congressional committee. In addition, she wrote a chatty, delightful newspaper column for thirty years called On the Trail. She also wrote two books of Gunflint reminiscences and co-authored another with Betty Powell Skoog, as well as make many tapes of oral history for the Minnesota Historical Society.

There were very few issues involving Gunflint country on which Justine was silent. The gradual disappearance of wildlife, continual road building, the clearcutting of the forest and many other topics have felt the Kerfoot lash. During the time of many wilderness bills considered by state and federal legislatures, including the establishment of the Boundary Waters Canoe Area and the subsequent buyout of private property, Justine, who opposed most of it, was a strong and strident voice. Her forte was participating in Congressional hearings and committee appearances on this subject.

Even sometimes opponents, such as Kevin Proescholdt, executive director of Friends of the Boundary Waters Wilderness, were in awe of Justine. In *Troubled Waters*, he describes her:

"But the most intriguing character of all was a five-foot engine of raw energy, will power and chutzpah named Justine Kerfoot, who defied easy categorization. She had lived along the Gunflint Trail since the 1920s. She had visited as many countries as BWCAW lakes. She could as easily charm an audience with her eloquence as she could embarrass a sailor with her vernacular. She had faced down bears, county commissioners and anyone else who got in her way. Even environmentalists begrudgingly admitted their fascination with her."

Justine died in June of 2001 at age 95. She was somewhat frail after several replacement surgeries and a few bouts with pneumonia, and often seemed to be dreaming of faraway portages. Before her final illness, I occasionally saw her standing near her cabin on the Gunflint Lodge grounds in her familiar red and black checked lumberjack shirt, her tight cloche of silver hair gleaming in the sun. She was probably smelling the piney air, checking the condition of her trademark red canoe resting upside down on blocks next to her cabin, or watching the waxwings and chickadees at her feeder—Justine Kerfoot: our Lady of the Trail.

Justine Kerfoot, "Our Lady of the Trail," died at age 95 in 2001. She had lived on the Gunflint Trail since the 1920s and always epitomized the strength and self-reliance of The Gunflint Woman. A resorter/businesswoman, fishing and hunting guide, trapper, newspaper columnist, world traveler, wife, mother and grandmother, congressional witness, author, lecturer, good friend and neighbor. Justine did it all.

Where the land slopes up from the narrows to form a notch in the horizon is where archaeologists sometimes look for evidence of the camps of Paleoindians who kept watch on the migration routes of the game animals they relied on for food.

CHAPTER 4

Beginnings:
Voices from the Glacier

The stories of the characters who people the Gunflint Trail and surrounding country represent one voice of this magical place. But before there were people—white or indigenous—there was the land.

It is now well established that in the mists of pre-history, approximately 10,000 years ago, after the Great Lakes Basin was entirely free of glacial ice, there was a group of Paleoindians, the first human occupants of the region. This ancient people camped along the north shore of Gunflint Lake and at the Cross River inlet at the west end and left only unintentional records of tools, weapons and decorations.

The Cross River enters the west end of Gunflint Lake placidly in a marshy bay after a ten-mile dash through boulders and beaver cuttings alongside the Tuscarora Road and the Gunflint Trail. The south side of the bay, at the river's mouth, is edged with willows, reeds, alders, rushes and wild rice. Then the land rises sharply for one hundred feet to a heavily wooded slate cliff.

The north side of the river has a completely different character than the south, with conifer and birch-covered shelves of basaltic rock rising gently from the river for a couple hundred feet to a long, storm beaten slope of sand terraces. U.S. Forest Service Archaeologist and Project Director, David Woodward speculates that the terraced deep sand is evidence of an ancient glacial lakeshore. Woodward has searched sites in Guatemala and the Yucatan Peninsula of Mexico for the National Geographic Society, the North European plain in northern Poland for the Polish Academy of Sciences and many sites in Wisconsin and Minnesota.

When he was surveying the Cross River for possible excavation, he found a siltstone multi-purpose tool on the ground and another of jasper taconite wedged into the gnarls of a white spruce root throw upended by the 1999 storm. He speculated that both of these are Paleoindian (10,000–6,000 years ago) artifacts, perhaps 8,000 years old.

This evidence inspired him to a more serious examination of the topography, and he theorizes that perhaps herds of caribou migrated this way in the post-glacial period when the vegetation was vastly different. The herds might have come down the slope from the north to the river, crossed around the end of the cliff at the lakeshore, then moved over their historic migration route on to the south over more level ground. The abundance of game would have beckoned indigenous peoples of three cultures to this spot on the migration route, making it an ideal location for a hunting camp. Perhaps it was one of these hunters who left his knife on the ground that Woodward found 8,000 years later tangled in upended roots. Sites like this are among the several thousand that U.S. Forest Service archaeological crews have found along the Boundary Waters.

On the third day of the Cross River Gordon Site dig (named for a Gordon's Gin bottle found under a stump), excitement ran high among the Passport in Time excavation volunteers, who manipulate their delicate instruments and work at their craft with the skill and concentration of emergency room surgeons. They probed down to the three-centimeter level with their tiny trowels, probes and picks on the sand slope site where they began to find pottery shards. No firm cultural date has been assigned to these artifacts and identification is speculative, but it is possible this pottery may be from around 500 BC. This was also the approximate time wild rice came into use as a staple food, so containers were needed for parching the rice for storage.

A Gunflint silica hide scraper was found in one of the excavations higher up the slope, which may be a Paleoindian artifact. At about the same level, archaeologist Sarah Crump came up with the jewel of the dig: an oval-shaped polished siltstone pendant with a neat hole drilled at top center from an as yet undetermined cultural period. On a chain or thong, this ornament would look quite elegant in any gift shop display case today.

Other finds in the sand slope excavations included several dart points, the lethal tips of jasper taconite that were attached to short spears, and the "power boost" devices used to increase the speed and accuracy of a projectile, used by late Paleo, Archaic (6,000–500 BC) and Woodland peoples (500 BC–1680 AD). The bow and arrow wasn't in use until the Woodland Period in the early AD years. A copper chunk of unidentified use also was found in this pit.

Volunteers Ulla Kendler and Mary Aimoniotis uncovered a jasper silica trihedral engraver, a six-inch long, three-edged tool used to work wood and bone.

At the 24 cm. level on this site, Nicole Lohman discovered a beautifully shaped and edged projectile point and Volunteer Margit Jamieson found a scatter of 133 stone flakes in a pile nearby in the same pit. These would indicate the excavation was in a work area where tools were being fashioned, possibly during the early Woodland Period.

The public is invited to these U.S. Forest Service Heritage Resources digs, and several hundred visitors registered at the exhibit tent at Cross River. Here, lectures are given on the current work, the artifacts displayed and the key elements of history's sweep from the retreat of the glaciers. A unique feature of the project is the guided tour for the public—conducted by an archaeologist or trained volunteer—of the entire site, during which the process of excavation and screening was explained and found artifacts examined. Ongoing through the tour is an overview lecture of the area's probable history.

By encouraging public participation in archaeological digs, the U.S. Forest Service is attempting a dramatic change in policy away from the traditional tight security and cordoned off locations that have been necessitated by the theft of artifacts, site defacement and other vandalism. This new concept is a facet of multiple use and the public ownership of Forest Service lands. The policy is based on the belief that inviting public participation, providing educational material and giving hands-on archaeological experience will encourage proprietary feelings about the site and its contents.

"An informed public is the best protection for a sensitive site," says Walter Oaksted, Superior National Forest Historian and Program Manager of Heritage Resources for the U.S. Forest Service. "By informing and educating we hope to create an awareness of our work and the sensitive nature of the site which will, in turn, provide the best protection over time."

It is now well established that in the mists of pre-history, approximately 10,000 years ago, after the Great Lakes Basin was entirely free of glacial ice, there was a group of Paleoindians, the first human occupants of the region, camped along the north shore of Gunflint Lake and at the Cross River inlet at the west end. Other camps have been found on the high palisades over Rose Lake, on the wooded shore of Watap Lake, at Campground Point on East Bearskin Lake and on the overlook on top of Pincushion Mountain above the present town Grand Marais, where the Paleos could have dangled their feet in Lake Superior, as it was 200 feet higher then.

Several sites in the Gunflint region have been excavated and identified as Paleo camps, and one of the things that puzzles and amuses Gordon Peters, the retired

Supervisory Archaeologist for the Superior National Forest, is that most of them are on extremely scenic spots, almost as though these Paleoindians were the first tourists to visit and enjoy the area. It is more likely, Peters concedes, that the sites were picked as the best spots from which to observe game.

"Protection from enemies is an unlikely possibility," he says, "because the concept of territoriality, or land ownership, was foreign to any Native American societies in the Arrowhead region until European migration and the fur trade era."

"Paleo" is a word science has borrowed from the Greek meaning "old," and is used in this context to designate the descendants of that group of aboriginal people who likely crossed the land bridge of Beringia from Siberia to Alaska during the Ice Age. Over the centuries, these people migrated across the ice-free Alberta corridor to this area where they hunted the woolly mammoth, giant beaver, saber-tooth cat, tapir, woodland bison, and other now-extinct Ice Age mammals that roamed the tundra and spruce forest that covered the opening land as the glaciers melted.

In fact, had the Paleos climbed a hill and looked to the northwest, they would have been able to see the retreating ice sheets which had been the dominant feature in this environment for centuries. The glaciers became stalled north of the Quetico, where they remained until about 8,000 years ago. By this time, the Paleo people were well settled all over the Gunflint region.

In *The Great Journey*, author Brian Fagan calls the Paleos "shadowy and ill-defined figures....Knowledge of Paleo Indian life is a matter of archaeological shreds and patches of clues obtained from excavations all over the Great Plains, but it is possible to build up a broad picture that accommodates the most reliable evidence....Archaeology gives no firm answer to when human beings spread south of the Wisconsin Ice Sheets. But it is likely that, as the glaciers retreated, hunters pursued big game animals along the ever widening corridor to reach the North American plains."

We don't know much about these Paleoindians of the Gunflint region. The 2.7-billion-year-old Canadian Shield, the stable nucleus of the continent, is just inches below the surface in most places, making burial unlikely, so the Paleoindian and his possessions quickly became a dusty secret of the North Wind. No skeletal remains have ever been found in the Superior National Forest, although some have been found at the Cummins Site near Thunder Bay, Ontario. The data of prehistory here is gathered from the "unintentional records" of tools, weapons, ornaments and old hearths or fire pits found in abandoned campsites or old root throws.

We do know these Paleoindians were the first to exploit the resources of this area ,but because of climate and habitat changes they failed to sustain themselves. Little by little the tenuous threads of evidence are being woven into a prehistorical tapestry by archaeologists working on the shores of the lakes, along the rivers and deep in the forests of the Gunflint region.

Archaeologist Peters, his professional associates, and the volunteers from Passport in Time, while searching a site on Campground Point of East Bearskin Lake a few years ago, made some tantalizing finds. Part of a fluted spearhead, a turtleback scraper and a crudely worked piece of native copper were unearthed near the surface of this site where only six inches of soil represented 8,000 years of use. The walls of the Bearskin fire circle exposed blackened rings, which indicated that this fire circle—built in a root throw where a big tree went down— had been used for many generations. A turtleback scraper of Hudson's Bay chert used to smooth the shafts of spears was also found. Peters identified its function by the cuts along the edges, giving the scraper a ragged edge that can dig out small branches and knots to make the shaft smooth. Had it been a hidescraper, the edge would have been smooth and even, like a knife blade, designed to cut out fat and hair without damaging the hide.

Some of the stone chips found here are of Hixton quartzite from the Black River Falls area of Wisconsin, which might indicate some migration of the people as there undoubtedly was trading among the many bands of Paleos in the upper Great Lakes region. They were a nomadic people and took their tools and weapons with them, following the game, trading and responding to climate changes. Their movements can be traced by the types of stones they used for implements.

"The important thing about the East Bearskin dig," according to Peters, "is that it has provided incontrovertible evidence of the early (approximately 8,000 BC) Paleo occupation of this area."

About a thousand people visited the three-week dig on East Bearskin Lake and when we joined Peters and his crew, there were one hundred excited spectators at Campground Point. Using whisk brooms, dust pans, small trowels and rulers, instead of the picks, shovels and screens usually associated with excavations, the crew meticulously separated and examined every teaspoon of earth in the thin layer of soil that produced secrets older than the Pyramids of Giza. The ten-by-ten-foot excavation area, which was only a few inches deep, looked more like a sodding patch than an archaeological dig. When an item was discovered, all digging stopped until a grid of ten-centimeter squares could be lowered over the location and the item "piece plotted" on a map of the area.

These Paleoindians who camped at East Bearskin, on the Gunflint shore and at the top of the Rose Lake cliffs were really quite short term residents. It is estimated that there may have been a total of only 3 or 4 hundred of them in the Gunflint region and their culture lasted only 3,000 years—a mere jot of geologic time. By 6,000 BC, the climate and habitat had changed and the red and white pines replaced the scrubby post-glacial, tundra-like forest. The game animals that were the subsistence of the Paleoindians dwindled as they migrated north, following the glacier's edge to extinction. So too, apparently, the Paleo people seemed to vanish down the dark tunnels of time.

Peters suggests these early civilizations of the boreal forest did not so much vanish as undergo lifestyle changes in response to habitat changes and that they survived in subsequent cultures with different technological traditions. Some anthropologists surmise that this hereditary coalescence of several Paleo groups eventually became part of the Archaic Culture of the New Copper Age, who were adapted to the new pine forests and the animal resources found there. They took advantage of this newly found habitat diversity, which lasted from approximately 5,000 BC to 200 BC, following the Paleoindians in the human culture drama of the Gunflint region.

A treasure of historic and prehistoric artifacts has been found in and around South Fowl Lake, the first lake north of the arduous nine-mile-long Grand Portage. Using this waterway were the Paleoindians, centuries of Copper Age and Woodland Culture peoples, the later Ojibwe and Cree, and then French, English and Scottish fur traders plying the Voyageur's Highway during the fur century. All used the relatively open areas, such as the "meadows" along the Pigeon between South Fowl Lake and Partridge Falls, and also the broad sand beaches of South Fowl Lake, as rest and preparation areas. The founder of Winnipeg, Lord Selkirk, established his first settlement here at the Meadows, but it soon failed and was deserted.

There is an island in South Fowl Lake that was used for the same purpose by at least three separate cultures spanning the 10,000-year history of this area. From the earliest occupants of the region—the Paleoindian people—collectors have found stone axes, mauls, flint, slate and jasper taconite spear points and hide scrapers. From the Copper Age there are spear points, dart points, knives, awls, spuds, fish hooks, jewelry and ornaments. The absence of arrowheads is explained by the fact that the bow and arrow wasn't used until after 1,000 AD.

52

From the Voyageur period of the eighteenth and nineteenth centuries, a variety of items has been recovered including muskets, trade beads, muskrat spears, knives, arrowheads, pewter spoons, cooking utensils, a unique silver candle snuffer, and a silver teakettle retrieved from the bottom of the rapids between Little Gunflint and Little North Lakes, several miles upstream.

Perhaps the most significant find of the1962 Quetico-Superior Underwater Research Project undertaken by Bob Wheeler, Associate Director of the Minnesota Historical Society and the Royal Ontario Museum, was the recovery of a nest of 17 complete brass kettles in nearly perfect condition taken from the plunge pool below Horsetail Falls on the Granite River near Gunflint Lake.

"This was a rare find," said Wheeler. "It hasn't been duplicated anywhere before or since. Surely it was lost by some unfortunate trader when his canoe upset."

Another productive site has been the broad sand beaches of the island in South Fowl Lake which used to be a peninsula. Actually, South Fowl Lake didn't even exist until 1900 when the Pigeon River Lumber Company built a wooden dam across a narrowing of the Pigeon River to raise the water level high enough to float logs and to provide a head of water for the drives down the river. This changed the entire shoreline and made an island out of the river bank peninsula. The logging company's dam was replaced by a more permanent concrete structure in 1930.

The archaeological site itself, which is now on the National Register of Historic sites, is underwater, and the artifacts found on the island's surface have been pushed there from the bottom by the turbulent movement of ice as it melts in the spring.

In their collection of copper and stone artifacts from this region, collectors Dick and Lou Anderson and their son Rick, of Grand Marais, found the prize of their collection: a 7,000-year-old socketed copper spear point with wood fibers from the shaft still imbedded named by the Minnesota Archaeological Society as the "Anderson Point." Dated at the University of Toronto, this spear point is the oldest fashioned metal artifact ever found on the North American continent.

The Anderson collection also includes other projectile points, knives, awls, needles, hammerstones, hide scraping tools and several ornamental items such as beads, bracelets, rings and pendants. Almost all the Anderson artifacts have been surface finds scattered on beaches and retrieved in the late spring.

One of Dick Anderson's fascinating finds was a disc of tightly coiled copper wire about two inches in diameter, about as old as Stonehenge, with the outer end bent into a slight bow. Anderson thought this might be half of an ancient version of snow goggles, the kind the Inuit people of the snowy, far Arctic regions made of wood or walrus ivory to reduce the blinding glare of sun on the snow. He thinks tight coils of wire with small holes in the center would accomplish the same thing for winter travel of snow-covered lakes.

Gordon Peters has another interpretation. "I've seen two identical double coils from Trout Lake, north of Lake Vermilion," he explains. "I think these are probably stylistic serpentine symbols that represent death. At least that is how similar symbols on pictographs (rock paintings), and Mide scrolls (Grand Medicine Society records) have been interpreted."

Anderson, retired president of the Grand Marais State Bank, is the grandson of the legendary Alexander Jackson Scott, and Catherine Boyer Scott, a French and Native American convent-raised woman from Fort William. He has inherited some of his grandfather's love of exploring the Gunflint region and its history. Both Dick and his wife, Lou, have enough Ojibwe blood to qualify them for membership in the Grand Portage band of Ojibwe, and this enables them to maintain a summer home on reservation land. Dick found his first artifact, a spearhead, thirty years ago when he accidentally turned over a rock right in front of his hunting shack on South Fowl Lake.

"Talk to me," whispers Lou Anderson, her eyes closed as she gently rubs the 5,000-year-old copper bracelet she found in the beach sand at the island in South Fowl Lake. There is a reverence in her voice; she is hoping to communicate with ancestors. A vivacious woman with the high cheekbones and dancing dark eyes that hint at her Ojibwe heritage, she is taken back in time, probing for hidden memories. She wants to know more about this bracelet, now pocked and abraded by the fine sands and the buried time of Anishinaabe centuries.

A very spiritual woman, Lou talks to every artifact she has collected. "Tell me your story," she implores each of them.

Also in the Anderson collection, which they have assigned to the Minnesota Historical Society, are many red jasper spear points with parallel, or Plano, flaking, identified as Paleo, nearly 10,000 years old—the earliest evidence of human occupation in the Gunflint region of northeastern Minnesota.

Betty Hemstad

Because of the rocks, ridges and valleys in the Gunflint region that create many varying altitudes, stream water always seems to be tumbling and racing. It is cold, clear water which would seem to be ideal for trout, but for some reason there don't seem to be any trout in the streams north of the continental divide, which crosses the Trail at Birch Lake.

Since 1854, which marked the opening of the rocky Gunflint region to settlement, it has been a favorite place for mineral prospectors and land speculators. Fortune tales of gold, silver, nickel, copper, iron, cobalt and titanium have circulated for years but nothing of marketable value has ever been found.

CHAPTER 5

Gunflint Minerals: A Ring of Riches

At the 1900 high school Commencement Day exercises in Grand Marais, valedictorian Maggie Scott addressed the graduating class with her visions of the area's future that were as bullish as they were wrong.

According to Ms. Scott, Grand Marais "would soon fulfill the wildest optimism," and that there would be "huge docks for ore....There will be ships, railroads and streetcars here...All that woods will be gone and in its place a large and noisy city."

A horror story? Not according to author/historian Willis Raff, who suggests in *Pioneers in the Wilderness* that "whatever the perspective of the reader in this century, Ms. Scott's dream represented the conventional wisdom of its time." In 1900 the entire county was "aflame with the wildest optimism, that right here, in the Gunflint region were great mineral fortunes waiting to be discovered and that with hard work and entrepreneurial vigor Grand Marais would soon be the Pittsburgh of the North," the industrial capital of the Great Lakes, as predicted by *Grand Marais Pioneer* editor, A. DeLacey Wood. These early dreams were much different from the way things turned out.

In America, this was the era of Manifest Destiny, a catchphrase implying the sanction of territorial development and exploitation at its most ravenous. As stated in *United States Magazine*, in June of 1890, "Our manifest destiny is to overspread the continent allotted us by Providence for the free development of our multiplying millions." The doctrine was interpreted by most to mean that all the nation's natural resources were put there by a Divine Hand to be used by us, His chosen people, for our sustenance and enrichment.

The entire Gunflint region was explored, drilled, excavated, probed, blasted, logged, burned and then left alone for decades to heal until President Theodore Roosevelt included most of the wounded land in the Superior National Forest he established in 1909. In a remarkable caprice of geological fate, the Gunflint region never produced a shovelful of mineral value, but was completely surrounded by a ring of incredible riches: the immense wealth and power of U.S. Steel, Toronto Silver and Kennicott Copper, mining the nation's largest iron ranges immediately to the west; great fortunes of silver near the Ontario borders to the east and north; and the active copper mines of Michigan's Upper Peninsula and northern Wisconsin just across Lake Superior to the south.

Before the tourists and the sportsmen, before the loggers and the farmers, before the surveyors and even before the ink was dry on the Treaty of La Pointe in 1854 which opened northeastern Minnesota to white settlement, the prospectors and land speculators came north with the glint of mineral riches in their eyes. They were bunched up on Wisconsin Point like sprinters at the starting line, waiting for the signal the treaty had been signed that would send them racing across Duluth Harbor to start staking claims on the abundant riches in gold, silver, copper and nickel.

Typical of the fortune seekers waiting to enter this land of great mineral wealth was Robert McLean, who wrote in September of 1854, "What conversations I heard around me all turned toward silver and copper claims. There were rumors of great masses of pure large veins full of copper that could be traced for long distances."

There were wonderful stories going around then, embellished by the feverish imaginations of the prospectors and fueled by news reports and the land speculators, of "ancient diggings" by native people of gold and silver, caches of knives, awls, projectile points and other tools of pure copper. In addition, rumors circulated that the Gunflint contained pure silver nuggets the size of duck eggs just waiting to be scooped up, plus giant boulders of pure copper, gold in white quartzite bands, and iron literally as common as dirt.

In 1885 Henry Eames, the state geologist, was leading a party to alleged gold fields in northeastern Minnesota when Christian Weiland, one of the party from Beaver Bay, noticed his compass needle's wild deflection. "We're standing on iron," he exclaimed. "To hell with iron," responded Eames. "It's gold we're after."

And with good reason: gold was the subject of most rumors and hopes. Several likely locations were being test mined in northeastern Minnesota during these years. The *Minneapolis Tribune* carried many stories of the anticipated bonanza up north. Typical was an item in an October, 1884 edition:

"Greene Pack...today invested heavily in gold lands in Lake and Cook County.

H.M. Land, and Pack, both wealthy men, will start mining camps at the gold fields at once. There will be 500 men in the camps by March or April."

And in a letter from Cook County Auditor John Millar to a friend in the State Capital:

"The gold and silver excitement increases....Some startling assays have been made....One party bought nearly 40,000 acres on the strength of them."

Gold Island near Red Rock Bay in Lake Saganaga at the end of the Gunflint Trail was the site of more gold fever in the 1870s, where men were frantically peeling off the side of a cliff that displayed a large white quartz band containing traces of both gold and silver.

A typical gold story appears in *Pioneers in the Wilderness*: "Old Joe Kadunce was a living legend in his time; he was able to make a good living despite never having any regular employment because everybody in Grand Marais believed he had a private gold mine somewhere in the woods. Once or twice a year the old timer would take off alone for the north country and return with enough gold nuggets to keep him for many months."

Another "lost gold mine" story that still has some credence among old-timers involved Chief Blackstone, head of the Saganaga band of Ojibwe and patriarch of the Powell family presently living on Saganaga. According to the legend, Blackstone found a huge gold nugget and presented it to the Royal Family of England. Allegedly, his mine was somewhere north of Cypress Lake and it is said that trapper Benny Ambrose spent much of his life on Cypress looking for that mine. When Benny first came to the region from Iowa, he settled in a cabin on MacFarlane Lake where he trapped the Grand Portage area. But later, according to Shirley Peruniak in her *History of Quetico Provincial Park*, "Benny chose Ottertrack because he thought he was close to the legendary gold of Chief Blackstone. He never did find it and the story lives on."

There were productive gold mines at Murillo and Seine River in Ontario, not far from the Minnesota border, so it is possible that nuggets showed up at banks and in cash registers on the American side.

In 1910, Otto Monsen tried interesting John Hammond of Duluth in backing a scheme that he claimed had worked out in the Black Hills of South Dakota, extracting gold from iron ore by the "cyanide process." Three pounds of cyanide mixed with one ton of water, sluiced through crushed iron ore would yield $3 worth of pure gold per ton of iron, he claimed. Monsen just happened to know where they could get a lot of iron ore that wasn't being used. There was plenty up near Gunflint Lake, but he never got any takers.

In 1931, the *Duluth Tribune* shouted, "Two Harbors Went Wild" when gold was discovered near the now ghost town of Cramer on the Cook/Lake County Line. As late as 1934 the fever was still raging. Again there were big headlines: "Rich GOLD Deposits on Canadian Side of Sag!" The "gold" turned out to be fool's gold, or iron pyrite, as almost all of it did. What was genuine had the same profile as all Gunflint "riches"—low quantity and poor quality.

After 70 years of poor geology and worse journalism, the chairman of the Geology and Minerals Department at the University of Minnesota, George Thiel, in *Minnesota Mineral Heritage*, finally wrote closure to the rumors of gold in northeastern Minnesota: "The Little American Mine in Rainy Lake was the source of the only gold production in Minnesota. It operated in 1894 and '95 and produced gold valued at $4,635.33.... Since that time many veins and gravel deposits have been test-pitted or drilled, but none has ever proven of any value."

For twenty years after the Gunflint region was opened to white settlers, these prospectors sweated, dug and blasted their way through most of the county, never making the Big Strike, but hanging on doggedly to their dreams. Occasionally something really big would happen to renew their spirits and give them strength to go on. There would be a teasingly hopeful assay from a geologist, then two incredibly rich silver strikes were made just across the Ontario border and the almost pure copper boulders on the Michigan Upper Peninsula just across the Big Lake created a few instant millionaires.

Here, just off the Gunflint Trail, Capt. William P. Spaulding was exploring the centuries old "mines," the Ancient Diggings near Greenwood Lake, which had been worked by early native peoples.

What were the secrets of these randomly dug pits? Gold, silver or copper? In *Copper Trails and Iron Rails*, Larry Massie reports that Sam Knapp, a Vermonter drawn to the Michigan Peninsula wilderness by the lure of mineral riches, discovered an ancient digging in 1848 that contained "large masses of native copper resting on a platform of rotting logs," which eventually became the misspelled Minesota Mine, one of the most profitable in Michigan copper mining history.

Almost three decades later, Spaulding spent several years at an ancient digging in the Gunflint region a few hundred miles north of Knapp's discovery, cutting roads through rocky hills, erecting a cabin and outbuildings, hauling machinery through wilderness bogs and digging long tunnels in a quest for silver or copper. Why this expenditure of several years of terrible labor at a remote site in the Gunflint woods? Could he have known about Knapp's good fortune, which had already become a part of mining history? There had been flaming newspaper headlines about his Michigan copper find in an ancient digging, several mining journals had covered the story completely and there were always the fortune tales of prospectors carried on the north wind.

But there is no written evidence that Spaulding ever knew anything about Sam Knapp's Minesota Mine or was driven by anything but his own demons to undertake this Herculean task. Alas, no silver, no gold, nor anything else was ever found and Spaulding mysteriously disappeared, never to revisit his "inexhaustible silver mine" near the Gunflint Trail.

Still, in 1869, an astonishingly rich lode of almost pure silver had been discovered on tiny Skull Island, fifty miles from the Minnesota border at the base of Thunder Cape in Lake Superior, now part of the city of Thunder Bay, Ontario.

In *Silver Islet: Striking it Rich in Lake Superior*, Elinor Barr says, "John Morgan stopped short at the water's edge and knelt quickly. Nuggets of pure silver winked back at him from their rocky prison. His unbelieving eyes followed the vein, a chalky white ribbon flecked with black patches of metallic silver that glistened invitingly beneath the ripples."

Bushels of the proverbial egg-sized nuggets were gathered off the surface of the island and a shaft dug which eventually reached 290 feet. Under the leadership of Thomas MacFarlane of the Montreal Mining Company, great fortunes in silver were taken from beneath this miniature island, which is only about the size of a baseball diamond. Stock in the mine went from $50 a share to $2,500 overnight and the mine produced handsomely for 12 years.

Coal was the key to the continuing production of the Silver Islet Mine. The shaft went straight down in the middle of the tiny island and seepage from Lake Superior could only be contained by huge coal-fired pumps running 24 hours a day. The coal was brought to the island by ship and in November of 1884, a load of coal was due which would keep the pumps running through the winter.

Unfortunately, it never got there. The allegedly drunk captain ran the ship aground off Houghton, Michigan, where it froze solidly into the lake ice. The pump fires went out at the mine, the shaft filled with water and the Great Silver Island Boom was over.

But there was good news, too. By 1880, another silver lode was being mined next door: the Great Silver Mountain near Whitefish Lake in Ontario, very near the Gunflint region and about ten miles east of Minnesota's Rose Lake.

Ron Brown tells the story of the 1884 discovery in *Ghost Towns of Ontario*: "Chief Joseph L'Avocat was so pleased with his daughter's engagement to Oliver Daunais he took him into his confidence and showed him the glittering streak of silver high on the windy plateau." That deposit, which stretched for over a mile, became the site of several mines that produced a high grade silver worth millions of 1888 dollars until the good ore ran out about five years later. But that wasn't the end of the Great Silver Mountain's contribution to the lore of silver mining. It was found that the lower grade crystalline cassite had several other uses. Eventually the highway to Thunder Bay was paved with it and by 1927 people claimed half the new houses in Winnipeg had been stuccoed with silver from the Great Silver Mountain.

The closest brush the Gunflint region ever had with mineral riches occurred when old Henry Mayhew—explorer, fur trader, prospector and real estate speculator—found iron deposits near the west end of Gunflint Lake in 1881. He didn't say much about it at first; he just filed his claims and kept his mouth shut. Perhaps like most prospectors here, he was preoccupied with more precious minerals, especially copper and silver. After finding iron in those rugged hills, he went back to the copper mine he had begun to dig at Spruce Creek near Lutsen, and also to a silver claim he had staked out in 1876, next to Spaulding's ancient diggings mine north of Greenwood Lake. He had gotten great reports on the Spruce Creek ore samples he had shipped to St. Paul and a big chunk of it was sent to the Vienna Exposition as an example of the great mineral wealth to be found in the wilds of northeastern Minnesota.

Mayhew's big problem was money. He had large land holdings in Cook County, but little cash and was depending on a consortium of Chicago speculators to bankroll his copper mining operations. But they grew weary of his claims for the region's promise, or perhaps the cost of tunneling into the cliffs became prohibitive. In any event, they withdrew their financial support and Mayhew abandoned the mine, but kept his Gunflint iron claim as a hole card and went back in 1881 to develop it.

Over the next several years there were many companies and individuals involved in attempting to mine the iron of the Gunflint, or Mayhew Range, but unfortunately, Mayhew and several others were aced out of their claims by large corporate interests and their lawyers who had invaded the region. By 1885, over 2,000 acres of the most promising iron lands on the Gunflint Range had been acquired by others.

The iron Mayhew had found was in a rugged triangle defined by the Cross River, the Kekekabic Trail to Ely and the Gunflint Wagon Road. A little city grew up near the mine site—called Gunflint City—and consisted of cabins, equipment sheds and a general store. Nearby was the saloon/brothel run by Meg Matthews, a Port Arthur brothel chain owner and the most famous madam in the North Country. Meg also entered regional history as the first recipient of a Cook County liquor license. She paid $500 for it in 1893.

In *Thunder Bay to Gunflint*, Ontario historian and author Elinor Barr, elaborates on the legend of Meg Matthews:

"Margaret 'Meg' Matthews of Port Arthur became a legend long before her death in 1937. She had established a reputation as a competent chef in1884 when she arranged an official banquet at Port Arthur's must pretentious hotel. Her brothels flourished, and her well known generosity to employees and down-and-outers suggests that a sizable sub-culture depended on her for social assistance."

Barr goes on to recount a story about Meg's popularity during World War I from J.P. Bertrand's *Timber Wolves*, a book of Northwest Ontario logging tales.

"A German soldier, who had undoubtedly been working in Northwestern Ontario, noticed the movement in and about the Allied trenches. He called out, "Hello, Canadians. Which regiment are we facing now?"

One of them replied, "The Lake Superior 52nd!"

"How's Old Mag?" was the response.

When Bill Raff led a group of local history buffs on an exploration of Gunflint's historic sites several years ago, they found, among other artifacts, two pairs of tiny satin slippers the ladies had apparently left behind when the town's economy collapsed suddenly and Meg Matthews' Gunflint brothel was abandoned.

Mayhew had discovered low grade ore, the far eastern tip of the giant Mesabi Iron Range. The mother lode was150 miles west in the Hibbing-Virginia area, so everyone but Mayhew picked up and deserted the Gunflint iron range, leaving machinery, two towns and Henry Mayhew's dreams to rust and crumble in the renewing forest. Although the railroad along Gunflint Lake's north shore was used for several years to haul logs and transport sportsmen, only one trainload of iron ore was ever taken out.

That was the end of Gunflint iron mining. During the short-lived boom a railroad had been built from Thunder Bay to the western end of Gunfint Lake. It was called the Port Arthur, Duluth and Western Railroad, nicknamed the Pee Dee, or as some irreverent residents called it, the Poverty, Anguish, Despair and Want. Most of the line on the American side was abandoned, but it was a modestly successful railroad on the Ontario side for some years hauling silver ore from the Rabbit Mountain mines and logs from the North Lake area.

To the south, a few hundred miles across the widest part of Lake Superior, miners were pouring into Michigan's Upper Peninsula and northern Wisconsin developing the richest copper deposits found to this date in the United States. It was known that the same forces of volcanism and the resultant lava flows had created the entire Lake Superior basin, so surely it would stand to reason that if there were huge copper deposits in the rocks of the Michigan Peninsula, they would also be present on the Minnesota side.

Raff says, "There had never been any doubt that the geological formations were the same." But was it possible that Cook County's economy would remain marginal indefinitely? No one could accept the gloomy idea that the area would continue "a sluggish backwater of America's (and Minnesota's) industrial progress."

The enthusiasm for Minnesota copper deposits sounded logical, but again it didn't work out that way. It has not been definitely established, but one explanation for the scattered diffusion of copper originating in magma from the mantle of the earth is offered by Ojakangas in *The Geology of Minnesota*. He and W. S. White conclude that "the steep dips of the lava flows on the Michigan side allowed hot copper-bearing fluids to move upward along porous flows...whereas the gentle dips of Minnesota's lava flows may have hindered such movement."

The concentration of copper on the Michigan Peninsula has resulted in billions of dollars of native copper being mined on the Upper Peninsula since it was discovered by French explorers in 1840, and the Upper Peninsula remains the only place in the world where copper in an almost pure state has been found in great chunks. From the excavation of an ancient digging near Ontonagon came a 500-ton boulder of pure copper—the largest single nugget of precious mineral ever found. Two of the largest mines in Michigan, the Hecla and the Calumet, were "discovered" by pigs rooting around in these prehistoric mine sites. Copper deposits have been found on Isle Royale off the north shore of Lake Superior area, but not much was ever found on the Minnesota side, except for thin veins of unmarketable ore in the Pigeon River area, used by Copper

Age peoples to fashion tools and ornaments.

There was another close call in the 1950s, and for a while it renewed the hopes for mineral riches in the Gunflint region. Russell Blankenburg, a resorter, entrepreneur, large landowner and amateur geologist, discovered a very promising vein of cobalt in a cliff at the west end of Loon Lake, just a few hundred feet from the Gunflint Trail in 1954.

It was an exciting and interesting find because there were no other cobalt deposits in the United States. Cobalt is a silvery-white metallic element used chiefly as a hardener for alloys. It withstands great heat, which makes it a useful component of jet engines, television sets, atom bombs, gas turbines and drill bits. Cobalt 60 is also used in radiation therapy to kill cancer cells.

Because of its scarcity and value there was a great furor about Blankenburg's cobalt discovery. More headlines. More excitement. More disappointment. The tunnel from which the first samples were taken was dug straight in from the cliff face. For a short while, all went well, but suddenly the miners were confronted by a blank wall of granite. It seems that there was a very large split, or fault, somewhere in the cliff's interior and a great huge section of it had slid down deep into the bowels of the earth. Unfortunately, it was the section that contained the remaining vein of cobalt. That was the last episode in more than a century of high hopes for mineral wealth in the Gunflint region.

If the anticipated mineral bonanza had been found, there would be none of the beauty, the majesty or the fulfilling richness of the region's natural gifts. Some still feel cheated by a capricious Nature that enriched surrounding areas by hundreds of billions of dollars, but others see it now as Divine Intervention, or just incredibly good luck that all those Gunflint shovels came up empty. No gold, no silver, no copper, no iron, no titanium, no cobalt. The Gunflint region, at the very center of the ring of riches was totally devoid of mineral wealth.

The road to the present for prospectors was a frustrating, labor-intensive and rocky one, full of hope and dreams of riches. Their bad luck and the escape from Maggie Scott's vision that "all those woods are gone and in their place a giant city," may be Nature's caprice but perhaps the Gunflint region's ultimate good fortune.

Minnesota Historical Society

At the trailhead, or southern region of the Gunflint Trail, the maple-aspen-birch-balsam forest prevails and the sub-boreal forest of pine-spruce-cedar-black ash is found on the northern end in the BWCAW. In between, there is a sprawling mosaic of forest communities, each with its own ecology.

CHAPTER 6

The Gunflint Forest:
A Work in Progress

Despite being approximately 10,000 years old, the Gunflint forest is still evolving. Fires, devastating wind storms, timber harvesting, climate changes, human uses and abuses, insect infestations, all have had continuing and dramatic effects.

Looking out over the forest from the vantage of the Gunflint High Cliffs, one feels this is a place of infinite peace, a landscape of silence and serenity. But the reality is that the entire forest area is ground under siege and the conflicts played out here are both natural and manmade. The swift and destructive convulsions of nature, such as forest fires or heavy wind storms, often wreak havoc in the forest. Slower, but equally destructive forces, such as insect infestations, have been occurring for decades.

One example has been the unprecedented 43-year infestation of spruce budworm in northeastern Minnesota, which has left many acres of the Superior National Forest patchy with ghostly gray spires of dead balsam fir and white spruce, especially visible along the Gunflint Trail. The best method of clearing the area of the gray and broken forest is the crushing technique the U.S. Forest Service is using. They topple the snags with bulldozers and crush the downed wood, encouraging the decomposition process and leaving clearings for new growth. While this leaves the forest patchy, this method produces results far better than the ghostly spires of dead fir and spruce which act as chimneys in a fire and scatter burning debris for acres.

Insect infestations were eliminated or cut short when fire was allowed to cleanse the forest and prepare it for renewal, but since the need to suppress fire has become a priority, the budworm invasions continue to erupt. The primary cause of this extended deforestation by the misnamed spruce budworm (balsam budworm would be more accurate) is the manmade change of the forest ecosystem, where fire suppression and logging have allowed the extensive proliferation of balsam fir, making the forest vulnerable to continuing budworm attacks. The timber industry contends the proximity of the unmanaged forests of the BWCAW and Voyageur's National Park serve as breeding grounds and an uncontrolled source of budworms.

Birds, such as the bay-breasted warbler and black-billed cuckoo feed on the budworms, and heavy rains during long, cool springs are the best natural weapons against the invasion since the Forest Service has wisely discontinued the use of pesticides and herbicides since1984. Future funding of new research may uncover some new treatment or controls, but currently nothing is being done to halt the budworm proliferation.

In spite of the assault on the aesthetics of the forest, Minnesota DNR Forest Health Specialist Mike Albers sees some possible advantages to the budworm invasion.

"Budworm plays a beneficial role in killing mature, overmature and deteriorating balsam fir stands," he said. "Outbreaks also benefit the forest by reducing balsam fir populations and encouraging other species. The budworm may be maintaining a healthy ecosystem by partially replacing the role of fire. Perhaps the continuous outbreak of spruce budworm could be viewed as evidence that there currently is more balsam fir than can be sustained in northeastern Minnesota."

When man enters the equation, battles drag on over longer periods of time. Loggers, legislators, environmentalists, mining companies, resort owners, recreationalists and government agencies—all forest stakeholders—have been battling over the natural and spiritual resources of the forest since the passage of the Preemption Act of 1841, the Timber and Stone Act of 1878 and the first Wilderness Bill in 1926. Veteran troops of all persuasions tire or retire, and another generation takes up the battle flag and charges forward. Only the battle itself remains constant, but the trump card remains in Nature's hand and occasionally it is played with a ruthless suddenness that leaves no room for doubt about who is really in control.

The Gunflint region is protected by the Sawtooth Range at its southern boundaries from the high Lake Superior winds that sometimes bring the Big Lake into the streets of Grand Marais, but occasionally it will be hit by violent storms, either straight line, high velocity windstorms that send downburst winds from as high as 20,000 feet; or tornadic, spiraling winds that slice through the forest in narrow, finger-like patterns. Most of these storms are quick, destructive and highly localized. Only once in living memory has the region experienced the sudden, powerful and destructive storm called by the National Weather Service, El Derecho (straight ahead)—a type of storm that exploded unexpectedly on the BWCAW and the Gunflint region on the Fourth of July in 1999. On the weather maps, the storm stretched from Fargo, ND to Thunder Bay, ON, but its most violent force was concentrated on the BWCAW and the adjoining Gunflint Corridor.

Shortly before 1 p.m. on that still, muggy Sunday, the forest around Gunflint Lake stood uneasy and waiting under a lowering sky. At noon I went down to the dock to get a better look at the eerie and alarming clouds churning over the lake. The Ontario hills across the lake glowed with the dark emerald of summer spruce, but as they marched off to the northwest all landforms blended into the same grayish, caribou-moss color as they faded into a steamy sky. The sky had been clear most of the morning, but now great ragged tatters of dingy clouds seemed to move in several directions at once across an opaque sky. The sun shone a coppery orange burnish in the southern sky, then a dirty slag of low, racing clouds blotted out all color.

Our cabin on the south side of Gunflint Lake is close to shore beneath the brow of a 200-foot-high ridge which effectively blocked much of the storm's approach. In what seemed like only a short moment our little world went from a gray, ominous stillness to a roaring dissonance of shrieking wind and splitting trees. From inside the cabin we watched the lake literally flatten out as the wind scraped the wavetops into spindrift and sent them swirling skyward in aurora-like veils.

A violent half hour later, great patches of the BWCAW and the upper half of the Gunflint Corridor forest were gone, the trees snapped off, thrown in jack-straw piles, uprooted, leaning, hanging or bent over to the ground. Although great patches of the forest were flattened, buildings and vehicles destroyed and possessions scattered, there were, remarkably, no fatalities. Several injured canoeists were taken out of the BWCAW by helicopter and the Cook County Hospital was busy for several days with broken bones, cuts and bruises.

John Henricksson

The Storm of the Century on July 4, 1999, brought 100-mile-per-hour winds and deluges of rain to northeastern Minnesota, and left much of the Gunflint region a grotesque landscape of flattened woods and thousands of trees snapped off about 20 feet from the ground.

The huge pines, spruce and cedar that went over in the storm upended their root throws, many of which were 30 to 40 feet in diameter. Because these trees often grow in areas where the bedrock is close to the surface they have no depth-seeking taproots to keep them anchored.

While standing in the parking lot at Trail Center a couple days after the big storm, surveying the jackstraw pile of trees and the big yellow machines already beginning the cleanup, owner Sarah Hamilton, a handsome, sturdy woman in bib overalls and boondocker boots, shook her head and sighed. "I know the forest will heal itself," she said. "But I'm not so sure about the people."

Now, after a few years, the forest is regenerating. Almost immediately, the U.S. Forest Service began clearing portages, trails and forest roads. County and states units opened other roads. Damaged cabins and outbuildings have been repaired.

New construction is evident all over the Trail, the fuel of downed trees is being burned and cleared and the people, with characteristic resilience, have responded to the disaster as a challenge. But fire—the rapacious fury of every forest—makes everyone wary.

Fire has raged through the Gunflint region since the first trees covered the newly exposed glacial drift. Dr. J. E. Potzger of Butler University, conducting research for his *Forest History of the Quetico-Superior*, recorded data from the peat sediments of the Little Long Lake bog and discovered that great fires inserted a "charcoal bookmark" into the pages of forest history. At the 16-foot level, he found such a marker that dated a large fire to approximately 3,500 years ago. Since then, similar bookmarks have been found as far back as 7,000 years ago.

For the past 400 years fires have been a prominent part of Gunflint region history. The Jesuit explorer/priest, Father Alneau, wrote to his superior in 1731 that along the boundary waters he and his companions "journeyed through fire and thick, stifling smoke which prevented us from even once catching a glimpse of the sun." In 1803, the Hudson's Bay trader J.D. Cameron wrote that "The whole country, almost from one extreme to the other was in continual blaze and was stopped only by the snows of autumn." In more recent history, great conflagrations have raged through the Gunflint region in 1860, 1870, 1894, 1910, 1923, 1926, 1929 and 1936.

In the past, forest fires were most often ignited randomly by lightning strikes, but as settlers moved into the area over a century ago, more and more fires were caused by man. The Native Americans started some to assist in harvesting game and to encourage the growth of blueberry and raspberry patches, but now half of the total fires are started by negligent campers, railroad fires, brush burning, sparking machinery, arson and careless smokers.

Extremely dry conditions and the buildup of fuels in the forest further increase fire danger. Lightning flashes sometimes ignite a tree and surrounding duff as it strikes, but more often will travel down a tree trunk into the root system where it smolders, sometimes for several days, before breaking out in flame.

There are fires in the Gunflint almost every year, and significant fires are expected any time, but the use of observation patrol planes, helicopters, tanker planes and the expertise of highly trained crews with better equipment and new technologies reduce the danger that a fire as big as those in the past will ever get a head start. When a fire does ignite and is reported, it is tackled immediately and is usually confined to relatively small acreage—but not always.

When a fire starts at night, especially in a remote area, and remains undetected for hours, and is carried on a rising wind, it can get away and become a major incident before mobilization is possible. This was exactly the combination of circumstances that resulted in the inferno called the Saganaga Corridor Fire of 1995, which burned 7,000 acres and cost $3 million to suppress. The best eye-witness description of that wildfire came from the Izaak Walton League's *Acorn*:

"All summer long, northeastern Minnesota baked under sunny skies as one gorgeous day piled upon another. No rain, aside from sporadic sprinkles, fell on the BWCAW for a month as the needle-carpeted forest floor became crispy, and dry, downed trees, slash and ground cover added fuel to the fire danger. In June, dreaded fires had popped up around Ely with others near the Gunflint Trail at Winchell and Swede Lakes, but these were swiftly controlled.

The big one, feared by all residents, flared up from an unattended campfire on Romance Lake, west of Lake Saganaga on August 10th. The conditions were perfect with 25–40 mph winds fanning the fire northeast into Canada. Firefighting forces of the U.S. and Canada attacked the uncontrolled blaze, which traveled five miles in the first few hours and eventually worked its way toward sprawling Northern Light Lake. In an uninhabited area, a fire would sometimes be allowed to burn and rejuvenate the disturbance-based forest, but this is a high use area with many resorts, residences and canoe outfitters, so an all-out effort was mobilized.

At the height of the fire, about 500 people were involved in the operation, with crews of 4 to 24 men and women, professional hotshots and volunteers work-ing to contain and control the fire, which was by then moving about one mile per hour. Experts from many areas were brought in, and some not so expert. A crew from Mississippi was assigned canoe duty to fight island fires, but they had never been in canoes before and capsized shortly after pushing off. Rappelling crews were brought in to fight the fires burning on the high cliffs.

The U.S. Forest Service, the DNR, crews from other areas, and the Gunflint Trail Volunteer Fire Department fought fires. The Cook County Sheriff's department, the State Patrol mobilized to control the heavy equipment traffic on the Gunflint Trail and keep curious onlookers away.

Helicopter pads were set up near the end of The Trail to service the eleven choppers that constantly darted across the sky, and 16 tankers carrying water from nearby lakes to douse the fires, were in the air all through the daylight hours. A tent city to house and feed firefighters rose in the large End of the Trail campground parking lot. Residents made thousands of cookies and doughnuts to accompany the gallons of coffee they supplied for the crews when they could grab a break. The smoke continued so thick it obscured the Canadian shore of Gunflint Lake, and after dark, a menacing glow lighted the entire northern sky.

Finally on the ninth day of the fire, nighttime thundershowers dumped an inch of rain on the thirsty forest, and put an end to the immediate danger, but the fire raged on for several more days across the Canadian wilderness."

Currently, with millions of storm-downed trees scattered on the ground serving as fuel, the forest is a potential cataclysm that haunts everyone in the area.

Still, after almost 100 years of fire suppression, fire is used now by the U.S. Forest Service to recycle nutrients and as a tool to clean the forest of downed trees, budworm snags, brush and other fuels that build to the danger point and inhibit new forest growth. Known generally by the term "controlled," or "prescribed burns," these fires have the official euphemism of "wild land fires used for resource benefit." Prescribed burning, which is ongoing along the Gunflint Trail, is one method by which the U.S. Forest Service hopes to eradicate part of the fuel buildup that could feed uncontrollable wildfires. Intentionally burned areas, such as the Lullaby Creek burn in 1998, are replanted. The Lullaby Creek burn was replanted with white and red pine seedlings, because the cone crop was particularly good in the previous year and now a beautiful new forest covers the land. The law now requires reforestation within five years of a cut or prescribed burn on all lands controlled by the U.S. Forest Service.

John Henricksson

The Saganaga Corridor fire of 1995 started by careless campers on Romance Lake left 7,000 acres of blackened tree trunks, but fortunately no lives were lost nor buildings destroyed.

But reforestation takes time. Several days after the Big Blowdown of 1999, and still in shock at the devastation around me, I asked forest ecologist Chel Anderson for information about the damage, healing and regeneration of the area. Chel has been working in this forest for 25 years, acquiring a thorough knowledge of its glories and its problems. She has worked as a forest management technician, a wilderness ranger and as a consulting ecologist to the U.S. Forest Service, The Nature Conservancy and the Minnesota Department of Natural Resources, and has lectured on all aspects of forest ecology.

"Chel, this is awful," I said. "The forest is gone."

"No, the forest isn't gone," she assured me. "I know it seems that way with all the shattered mature trees lying around. But the storm wasn't like a big forest fire that wipes out everything down to bare soil and rock. Only the canopy is gone and that's what makes it look so devastated, but most of the forest is still there.

"The understory and the ground cover survived and all the soil microbes, dormant seeds and sunlight are working to bring us a brand new forest. And it is already growing. You can see the subcanopy of unaffected young aspen, birch, balsam and spruce growing fast, now that they have no shade above them, and they will dominate for a long time. Their dominance is the big change you will see for many years."

"But will it be the same forest?"

"Almost, but not quite," she replied. "The same species and their interdependent relationships are still there. The pattern of the forest mosaic has been changed somewhat. By that, I mean the natural communities will be dominated by different species than before and will be of a different age and size, particularly in the areas of big pines that were blown down. I'm afraid those pines are gone for the foreseeable future. It is unlikely there will be any natural renewal of those groups, but the essential mosaic will still be there. The good news is that the subcanopy survived, and the white spruce, aspen, birch and balsam fir are shooting up in the open areas."

Ecologists call the Superior National Forest a mosaic—a unique intermingling of species and communities. The region is a blend of two forest types: the boreal forest and the eastern, or temperate, deciduous forest. The blending of these two forest types creates a more diversified community than is present in either type alone.

Natural communities composed of the species associated with both forest types have been here for close to 10,000 years. This medley of species within the two forest biomes creates serpentine invasion routes at the edge of each others' ranges blending to form a wide variety of native plant communities and habitats. These are dispersed across the landscape in a complex pattern that, when mapped by satellite, look like an abstract painting or a swirly, tie-dyed tapestry. New York State's Adirondack Forest, in combination with the forests of northern New England, is perhaps the only other temperate zone forest mosaic in the world near this size and diversity.

A month before the Storm of the Century, Chel had agreed to let me tag along on one of her survey trips along part of the popular Kekekabic Trail—the 40-mile hiking trail between the Gunflint Trail and Ely—where the composite of forest communities is at its most distinctive.

We loaded notebooks, field guides, bug dope, water, gorp and rain gear into fanny packs and started off down the trail, which originally was hacked out of the forest as part of a supply route for a series of fire tower lookouts. The upslope entry to the needle-covered path, from the Gunflint trailhead, is a boreal forest community of jack pine, birch, white spruce and black spruce, which was probably our first resident tree, as it colonized the recently exposed lands at the edge of the receding glacier.

The spruce trees, or "stands of origin," as the foresters call them, were festooned with great scarves of *Usnea*, or old man's beard lichen, which the parula warblers use almost exclusively for nest material. Off to the left and down a sharp, rocky drop is a little wetland filled with arum, or wild calla, with its shimmering, heart-shaped leaves and bright yellow spadix—a fleshy spike at the center of the pure white blossom.

There are also clumps of blue flag growing here from which, Chel said, the Native Americans made candy and with which, naturalist Sparky Stensaas says, they rubbed their nets to lure fish. The rocks are covered with the wiry reindeer, or caribou moss—a grayish lichen (from the Greek, for *leprous* or *scaly*) that has thousands of tiny branches giving it an ability to hold half its weight in water. Native American women used this lichen to line their tikanoggins (Ojibwe: *dikinaagan*), or cradle boards, when carrying their babies around on their backs. It is nature's most efficient and absorbent diaper material.

At the top of the rise, just a hundred feet away from a little pond, the land drops off sharply to a northeast facing slope that contains quite different plants than the landscape surrounding the slope.

"This is a fragment of the pure boreal forest community, which prefers this slope for its Arctic memories," Chel explained. "Under the jackpine and birch canopy of this grove, you'll notice there is a carpet of boreal plants clinging to the slope that would usually be found much farther north. If this slope were facing west, there would be entirely different plants here. Take a good look at the low ground cover plants: bishop's cap, lingonberry, goldthread, and farther downslope, the Labrador tea. These are Arctic species and usually dominate a community like this." Along the south edge in a grove of jack pine, the ground was dotted with the nodding pink blossoms of the pipsissewa, or prince's pine.

Crossing a long piece of the pinkish 350-million-year-old granite from the Saganaga batholith, Chel explained the little world that colonizes rocks like this. I spotted a tiny bouquet of bright red blossoms, the whole clump about the size of a dime. "These are British soldier lichens," Chel told me, "and are named for the red cockade of British colonial army headgear."

"It isn't really a blossom," she continued. "The scarlet knob on top of the half-inch stalk is the fruiting part. Its Latin name is *Caledonia cristatella* and it grows in sunny places such as on this granite slab, in soil or even on wood. By the way, it is another of the Arctic species found here."

The next forest community we entered was about a quarter of a mile down the root-veined trail and was dominated by a several acre stand of quaking aspen, locally called "popple."

Because of extensive logging, these trees dominate almost 30 percent of the forest now, but were much less common before the country was settled. In this grove, the tall aspens were all about the same size, or "even aged" to Chel, which would indicate that a disturbance, either logging or forest fire, had preceded their growth.

The understory of mountain maple, hazel, thick stands of balsam, and the occasional mountain ash created an impenetrable screen about ten feet high. The especially lush herbaceous layer, sometimes called the Canadian carpet, consisted of clintonia—each with three, pale yellow lily blossoms that would be replaced by dark blue berries in the late summer; twisted stalk, a relative of the prolific Solomon's seal; the pallid spikes of spotted coral root, a member of the orchid family; wild sarsaparilla, which, according to lumberjack legend, provided a decoction made into root beer; fleecy-leafed meadow rue; large leaf asters, wood ferns and the nodding pyrola.

A little farther down, past the test pits of the old Paulson mine, the trail dipped into a totally different micro-habitat: a dark grotto, the north side a wall of black basalt, made shiny with water seeping from the cracks in its surface. On the rock face was a profusion of rock polypody, a small evergreen fern, 4 to 10 inches long—a primitive plant with reddish spots on the undersides of the fronds. We had seen some wolf's claw clubmoss and horsetail, or equisetum, at the edge of the grotto, and I knew these were also primitive plants, but I wondered if that meant they were the first ones to appear here following glaciation.

"Nope," said Chel. "It means that their evolutionary history can be traced back in time to before the glaciers appeared. The first vegetation to follow the retreating glacier here was probably black spruce, willow and white birch. Black ash was also an early colonizer and is the only member of the ash family that remains in this area because of its ability to withstand our weather extremes."

Toward the end of our hike as we were resting on the slopey side of Hermit Rock on the shore of Mine Lake, I marveled at the diversity of habitats and species along the Kekekabic here in this small segment of the forest. I was sure that this indicated good health, so I asked Chel if my observation was correct.

She hesitated a little bit before answering. "The forest was originally very diverse. When the settlers came, the forest contained a healthy mix of age, species and diverse natural communities of birds, plants, mammals, insects and amphibians. Much of this still exists, but the more depleted the diversity is, and the more homogeneous the forest becomes, the more unhealthy it becomes."

"For the past 25 years there has been an intentional decision to manage the forest for aspen," she said. "This has benefitted two sectors of the wood products industry that use pulp, but not the forest as a whole.

"Today the forest is managed primarily for commodities. Even the forest mammals are an exploited commodity, but management is a given now. The effects of our presence and choices are happening whether we want them to or not. What we can do is make different choices, now and in the future, that will reflect other values of the forest, too. We must keep in mind that protecting the land means that we don't allow its use to outstrip its capacity to restore itself."

Checking the bird population and its habitat, which Chel had mentioned as one of the prime indicators of forest health, seemed to be the best way to start, and having participated in the Boreal Birding Weekend sponsored by the Gunflint Trail Association for the past several years, I had become hooked on birding. In the habitat seminar, which focused on forest health in relation to the bird population, I was particularly impressed with the facilitator, Janet Green, author of *Birds and Forests*, and former director of the National Audubon Society.

Seated in the comfortable living room of Green's handsome forest home about 20 miles northeast of Duluth, I was fascinated by the view. A wall-sized window looks out over a splendid "bird garden," planted with species of indigenous plants, whose blossoms and seeds attract resident and migrant birds. Occasionally, there are a few other visitors from the close growing stands of aspen, birch, spruce, sugar maple and pines surrounding the house.

"Hope you don't mind the bear slobber on the window," Janet apologized. "I'm running a little late this morning and haven't had time to wash that off yet."

Bear slobber? It seems a black bear, who visits Green's frequently, ambles into the garden after checking out a nearby swamp, walks upright past the side of the house, licking and investigating everything in sight, including the picture window, looking around for the bird feeders, which are uniquely designed to tip shut if anything bigger than a bird tries to get at the seed.

The garden in front of the big window is a bird smorgasbord of flowers: salvia, a blooming sage, and bee balm for the ruby-throated hummingbirds who are constantly zipping around the garden after Memorial Day. It also attracts spring migrants like Tennessee warblers who are on their way to nesting ranges farther north and then revisit the garden during the fall migration to the south in August. White-throated sparrows find the garden debris irresistible in the fall as well.

When I asked about the effects of the Big Storm on birds and their habitat, Janet was apprehensive but reassuring.

"The diversity of the forest mosaic is essentially unchanged," she said. "So I don't expect any major population shifts or sharp decreases, but the blowdown was so severe and covered such a large area that it will take a long time, 10 or 15 years at least, and a lot of work and money to fully assess the damage to wildlife and wildlife habitat. It may even be a boon to some, such as the black-backed woodpecker, our most nomadic species, which is always looking for fire or wind damaged trees.

"Some of the canopy nesters such as golden-crowned kinglets, vireos, purple finches, Blackburnian and black-throated green warblers may decrease. You seldom see them in new forests.

"Our bird population here in the Superior National Forest is unique in the country because we have the largest number of breeding bird species of any area north of the Mexican border. We have at least 22 species of warblers," she continued. "We don't have the most birds, you understand—that distinction belongs to states in the Corn Belt—but we have the most breeding species of any National Forest. Of those 151 breeding species here are 29 residents; 56 continental, or short distance migrants; and 66 neotropical, or long distance migrants.

"Most of the birds will be able to adapt, especially those species like wrens, sparrows and warblers who like young, brushy habitats. The numbers will change, but not drastically enough to affect the number of species. Most birds are site-faithful unless the forest is obliterated. If they come back in the spring to a burned or damaged forest, they will still find nesting places there and the young will disperse."

"Perhaps an even bigger problem right now is our management of the forest. The best stewardship of public land is to emulate nature, including disturbances, in order to maintain forest diversity, which is the key to bird diversity. For example, the shrubby aspen cuts are a favorite habitat of the chestnut-sided warbler, but we also need conifers and legacy structures such as snags, root throws and downed trees for winter wrens, flycatchers, and the rare three-toed woodpeckers.

"The dead aspen snags are especially attractive nesting spots to the boreal owls and the other 32 cavity dependent species here. We need the restoration of white pine and white spruce for the ospreys and bald eagles that nest near the tops of these big trees."

In her book *Birds and Forests*, Green states "it is this species richness that reflects the high diversity of habitats," and she gives reasons for using birds as accurate indicators of forest health in ecosystem-based management: Bird diversity allows for an accurate measure of ecosystem integrity because birds are visually and aurally conspicuous and thus easier to study; birds have a vital role in the functioning of the ecosystem because of their diet of seeds, insects and other bird's eggs. She also points out that they now have a public constituency that is rapidly expanding: two million people in Minnesota either feed birds or are active bird watchers, according to the U.S. Fish and Wildlife Service.

"Although we cannot measure effects with preciseness, forest fires, windstorms and logging cause some disruptions of bird population and habitat," Janet added.

"With the damage the forest sustained during the Big Storm, we mustn't miss this opportunity to study blowdown areas carefully. Also, and this is important: we now have the opportunity to perpetuate our native bird population and simultaneously produce forest products. It doesn't have to be one or the other. Some types of logging can be beneficial, but not the continuing increase now planned for the Superior National Forest region."

Most of the controversy about the management of the Superior National Forest swirls around the U.S. Forest Service, the statutory arbiter and authority. Their congressional mandate is to manage this landscape for multiple use. The National Park Service, the other major authority in the controversy, has a dual mission of preservation and human enjoyment. In that rather superficial distinction lie the flashpoints that ignite most of the controversies.

Superior Forest Supervisor, Jim Sanders, gives all petitioners his close attention. Sanders, a 28-year veteran of the U.S. Forest Service, has filled a variety of positions in the Gallatin and Clearwater National Forests as a biological scientist, forester, timber sales specialist and supervisor in addition to being the Forest Service liaison to the U.S. House of Representatives in Washington, D.C. for several years.

"A primary part of the Forest Service's mission is to provide an even flow of multiple resources," he says. "This includes all the resources of the forest: timber, clean water, recreation, minerals, wildlife, wilderness, diversity—everything the forest produces.

"Even though we are currently spending much of our time, money and effort dealing with storm damage cleanup, evacuation procedures and fire prevention, we have to keep our long range goals in focus. We must pay more attention to outcome rather than output.

"The Gunflint Corridor is a good example of an area that benefits from multiple use to maintain that area's vegetative character and appeal. What I want to see there along the natural area sandwiched in on the edge of the Boundary Waters is continued developed recreation, which gives a more complete wilderness experience; logging and prescribed burning to continue the forest's disturbance based character; more big white and red pines; forest conditions that will absorb disturbances; continued biologic diversity and more longer lived tree species."

Even though I am impressed with Jim Sanders' management and professional skills, I am well aware of the reality that regardless of his stewardship, the federal administration and the U.S. Congress are the ultimate decision makers and their judgements are often motivated more by politics and money than by forest diversity and health.

Demographics may seriously affect the forest's future. Dr. David Zumeta, who has spent the better part of a career in forest planning for the Minnesota DNR, and is now executive director of the Minnesota Forest resources Council, foresees continuing changes for northeastern Minnesota's forestland.

"I think what we're seeing is a gradual shift in the National Forests away from timber harvesting and toward placing more emphasis on the recreational aspects of forest lands," he says. "Today there is only about one third of the timber harvesting in national forests there was in the '60s. The Superior National Forest is not one of the great timbersheds of the country, like the western forests, but I think harvest levels will drop here as it has in National Forests around the country.

"I think this is due in large part," he continues, "to the fact that the demographics of these areas are changing so rapidly. Retiring baby boomers, second home owners, the growth of resorts, the businesses that service these groups and eventually, the political shifts that accompany changing demographics, will combine to change the social and economic climate of northeastern Minnesota."

The din of battle will likely continue as the various forest stakeholders review and renew their positions, adjust their agendas and push forward. The forest hopefully will endure in its wild grandeur.

The Devil Track river makes its peaceful winter way to Lake Superior through the Maple Hill outskirts of Grand Marais, ducks around Pincushion mountain and plunges into the 200-foot volcanic red rhyolite chasm on the Lake Superior Hiking Trail before flowing into the Big Lake.

CHAPTER 7

Gunflint Weather:
"A sumptuous variety, a dazzling inconsistency."

—Mark Twain

Millions of years ago, when the world was very young and the Gunflint region was on the shore of a tropical sea, marine crocodiles and sharks prowled the shallow ocean over what was to become the Gunflint region. Weather then would have been very predictable: endlessly hot and humid days in a tropical, swampy landscape. Eons and epochs later, The Gunflint would be in an opposite but equally predictable state, as grinding 1,000-meter-thick sheets of glacial ice covered the region in the silent deep freeze of the Pleistocene (Ice Age).

Since the glaciers melted back and a major climate and habitat change has occurred, the region has settled into a sometimes predictable northern temperate zone series of weather patterns with four definite seasons and a more amenable climate. Weather continues to be a major topic of conversation, but now everyone is better informed.

Getting current, accurate weather information any time of night or day has become easy now. The new, inexpensive weather radios bring instant reports and local forecasts from the Duluth station of the National Weather Service. This is all quite new. Before, we had to rely on forecasts usually presented by people hundreds or thousands of miles away who were looking at the big, big picture: air masses, fronts, occlusions and such, moving across great continental or oceanic sweeps with little attention paid to the topography or content of the landscapes they were passing over. Seldom were these forecasts very accurate because the weather of the Gunflint region never held still for this sort of atmospheric generalization.

For example, it is well known that nearby Lake Superior, the largest body of fresh water in the world, can make its own sudden and unreported weather systems, which it often does with dramatic swiftness and results.

The meteorologists in Atlanta or New York don't seem to know that here in the Gunflint region, the smoke is rising straight up from cabin chimneys, gulls are walking on the beach (not flying as they usually do), crickets have been chirping faster and dogs have been eating grass. But anyone whose life or livelihood relies on "weather sense," that is, knowledge of approaching weather systems, knows how important these observations of natural phenomena are. Many are just "old sayings," and have no validity but others have a solid scientific base and have proven useful for centuries.

This homely art of forecasting the weather by the observation of natural phenomena—part folklore and part science—involves weather lore and a single observer forecasting without instruments or foreknowledge of the weather. Native Americans, farmers and seafarers are its original and shrewdest practitioners. University of Minnesota professor of atmospheric physics, George D. Freier, explains the scientific principles behind the valid old sayings, many of which he has collected since boyhood on his Pierce County, Wisconsin farm home.

"Each proverb is a short, salty, common sense statement," he says. "Collectively, they cover the observations of many generations of people struggling with the weather." Freier doesn't claim these proverbs show greater accuracy than the "TV guys," but he is convinced of the scientific soundness of many of the proverbs.

In the preface to *The Wonder of Weather,* Freier says, "Throughout the centuries people have had to learn to cope with the weather to survive. They soon learned that plants and animals managed to cope with the weather through many diverse mechanisms. These mechanisms were often sensitive responses to weather changes. By watching plants and animals, people could often foresee what tomorrow's weather might be. To survive, folks had to observe nature more closely than most of us do now. Their discoveries and experiences were summarized in what we call proverbs."

He finds that 90 percent of the short range forecast proverbs have bases in scientific fact. "Weather information does not have to cease when we're in the woods," he continues, "if we know how to make a few observations of our own. Many things in nature are more sensitive to weather than we are."

Because many of the accurate proverbs are short range, they deal only with weather conditions of a few days, which is the average time it takes a weather system to move across the country. He thinks long range forecasts are bunk. "At the present time, we have insufficient knowledge about the physics of the atmosphere to make such predictions," he says.

A good example of an ancient and accurate proverb that has stood the test of time is found first in the New Testament and has come through the centuries in virtually the same words, still used by many to predict coming weather. Matthew XVI: 2–3 says,

"When it is evening, ye say, It will be fair weather for the sky is red. And in the morning, It will be foul weather today, for the sky is red and lowering."

Centuries later, mariners still claimed,

"Red sky in the morning, sailor take warning. Red sky at night is a sailor's delight."

And later, in medieval Wales they said, *"Evening red and morning gray send the traveler on his way."*

All are essentially the same weather advice, and all are based on a single scientific fact that is as applicable today as it was in New Testament times: the concentration of moisture in the air near the horizon makes the sun glow red and as weather systems move from west to east; this evidence of evening atmospheric moisture is a herald of rain. Sunrise redness in the east would indicate the moisture had passed. Because of all the pollutants we have in the air now, which often turn horizons red with the lowering sun, this proverb is probably not as dependable as it used to be.

One of the oldest weather proverbs on record comes from the Greek Theophrastus in 300 B.C., who states *"Ants run straighter as the temperature rises."* Dr. Freier's explains that "ants usually go in a straight line before it rains because they lay down a trail of pheromones so that other ants can follow them. When these substances become hydrated with moisture molecules from the air, they make for a more distinct and straighter trail."

Another weather proverb with sound scientific credentials, which has been used by seafarers for many years is:

Seagull, seagull, sitting on the sand,
It's a sign of rain when you're at hand.

This was followed faithfully for years by the commercial fishermen of Lake Superior who had a real need to know because their lives literally depended on their ability to judge weather. One thing the old lake fishermen did was keep their eyes on the gulls. They always checked to see if the gulls were flying or walking before they went out in their small boats. The gull is a soaring bird that needs updrafts under its wings. The thinning of air density during periods of low pressure lessens the natural updrafts that keep them aloft, so if the gulls were walking or perching on the beach, the fishermen turned to shore chores. Another piece of weather lore sailors and fishermen carried constantly in their memory is:

Mackerel scales and mare's tails
Make lofty ships carry low sails.

This means that when those long, feathery bands of high, cirrus clouds are seen during periods of low pressure, there are high winds aloft, which usually herald an approaching storm.

Those who spend their days outdoors need to know what kind of weather they can expect, and many use these proverbs even now with great confidence. Some of the favorite proverbs in this region with sound scientific bases are:

Waterfowl fly higher in clear weather. Ducks and geese will fly higher in the sky on fair days and closer to the ground on cloudy days. Observers can expect a stretch of clear weather for the next 14 hours or so.

When the wind is in the east, weather's no good for man or beast. This is an old English proverb and a forerunner of our useful but gloomy forecast that when a steady east wind blows, two days of unstable weather are almost a certainty.

Smoke rising from a cabin chimney means fair weather. Low pressure forces smoke downward and signals a change in the weather. My grandfather used to insist that a storm makes its first announcement down the chimney.

A ring around the moon means rain is coming soon. Pay attention to this advice! That ring is made of moisture particles and they are on their way, either as rain or snow.

If the North Star twinkles we will have rain. In Paul Deinhart's *Research Briefs*, he says, "Stars twinkle when there is turbulence in the air. You can see this effect when hot air rises from a chimney. Turbulent air is unstable and unstable air makes clouds, and clouds make rain."

Trout jump high when rain is nigh. When pressure is low, bubbles expand and stir up decaying material which minnows feed on and which, in turn, are chased by the trout.

Campfires are more smoky before a rain. "The persistence and visibility of smoke is also a sign of high humidity. As water evaporates from the particles, smoke turns blue because the particles are so small they scatter only blue light," Freier states.

Professor Freier, whose two weather books, *Weather Proverbs* and *The Wonder of*

Weather, cautions that weather lore often fails when it attempts to predict for long periods in just a few words, but woodsmen around here claim that the bears are good long range weather forecasters. They say that when a bear hibernates deep with a lot of sticks and grass in his den, it usually means a very cold winter without much snow. A shallow, barren, north-facing den is an almost sure sign of heavy snow because snow, a good insulator, will pile up at the bear's front door and keep him toasty.

Freier also warns of the easy deception of "hindcasting," or the observations that tell us more about the preceding year than the coming one. A good example of hindcasting would be basing a forecast of a hard winter by observing the thickened pelts of beavers or squirrels. This only means the previous year has been a nutrition rich one for the critters, says Freier. Another common proverb says that when the muskrat builds his cattail house high and bushy in the swamp, it means a hard winter is coming. Freier says it more likely means that the previous year produced a bumper cattail crop! One we often hear suggests that if we have a good year for blueberries—a bear's favorite pre-hibernation bulk-up snack—a long winter is coming. Not so. A lot of blueberries only means that spring sun and rain arrived at just the right time to produce a lush berry crop.

In an interview with the *St. Paul Pioneer Press*, Freier stated that he felt "common sense was a commodity largely nudged out of weather forecasting since farmer's firsthand observations gave way to computers and radar. The common man is often a better observer than those who sit in rooms with air conditioning and artificial light," Freier says. "We've become lazy. We don't observe nature like we used to."

One of the best of the natural science weather gurus was my neighbor Orville Gilmore, a man of a scholarly and inquisitive nature, who believed implicitly he could do a more precise job of weather forecasting for our region by the close observation of nature and by the careful use of his senses than any distant meteorologist with millions of dollars worth of equipment and little sense of geography.

If I wanted to go fishing or berry picking, I would always ask Orv the day before my jaunt what the weather was going to be like, and he never once misled me. I wanted to know more about this consistent accuracy and he graciously consented to an interview about the "Gilmore Flawless Forecast."

Wind direction and its strength are the key elements in his system, I learned. When he awakes in the morning, he lies in bed concentrating on the sounds of the wind in the trees and on the lake. All the sighing, humming, howling, keening and whispering across every surface and landform are meaningful to him and are the first things he analyzes. A proper interpretation of these sounds tells him all he needs to know about the coming weather.

When I asked him to explain the system further and teach me to use it, he agreed, but insisted, "Remember that my observations are valid only from my bed. Half a mile down the lake, or even at your place, the wind, the trees and the water all talk a different language, one that I would only partially understand.

"If I hear waves lapping gently on the rocks along the shore and the dock, but hear no wind in the trees, I surmise an east breeze. Since Gunflint Lake tilts slightly to the east-northeast, Hestons' Point and the hills beyond block the breeze and only the tails of the waves drag along shore. A steady east wind in the summer suggests two or three days of rain.

"A west wind, on the other hand, may rush through the trees along the shore dashing the waves against the rocks in long surges crashing like ocean swells. A west wind will likely send huge whitecaps rolling down the lake clearing and drying the air. We will probably be in for fair weather and a three day blow.

"North winds don't amount to much in the summer and won't last long before they veer to the east (rain) or to the west (fair), but they do have their effects: a constant lapping of waves, a steady sighing breeze in the trees and gusty rushes of cold air.

"If the wind gusts and rushes through the tops of the big pines and aspens, but the water along shore is silent, I expect a south wind to bring us an eventual thunderstorm."

I tried the Gilmore Flawless Forecast several times, but never got it quite right, so I went back to the master to see what I was doing wrong.

"It's because you sleep in a bedroom," he said. "In order to get it just right, you have to sleep on the porch like I do."

Providing observations, common sense and accurate weather data for the Gunflint region has been a second career for Fred Dell—a tall, silver-haired gentleman, who looks more like a retired diplomat than a veteran northwoods weather observer for the U.S. Forest Service and the National Weather Service. Fred worked for the Forest Service & NWS for 30 years, so I asked him how he came to be a weather observer.

"I think it was probably a matter of them not having anyone to gather consistent hard data about weather in this region. After all, they had no weather station anywhere around here. They needed a full-time, day and night weather observer," he says. "It stands to reason that if they have daily reports on temperature, wind, precipitation, barometric pressure, and all the other data they need for a forecast, they can be much more accurate—especially if that person has a well developed weather sense. But, they don't call it weather sense anymore. They have given it the euphemistic title of 'weather chronological instinct.' That's what I provided them—weather chronological instinct. That, and a pile of weather data every day and night for 30 years."

This daily observation of weather phenomena over a long period of years develops the sense Dell calls "weather instinct"— the ability to make complete and valid short range forecasts. "I even amazed myself with how accurate I became," Dell says. "If my wife Jenny would say she had to go to Grand Marais grocery shopping on Wednesday, I would say, 'No, you better not plan on that because we are going to get a storm on Wednesday.' And, sure enough, on Wednesday we would get a beaner of a storm."

Dell never felt comfortable making long range predictions, but he often admired the ability of the Ojibwe in the region when they would begin speaking confidently in July of the weather they could expect during the coming winter. "And, they were almost always right," he says. He feels this indefinable sense for approaching weather is a learned skill handed down through many generations of native people who depended for their lives and livelihood on their ability to sense coming weather.

One of the things that fascinates Fred Dell about Gunflint weather is its many vagaries and eccentricities within the 60 miles from the shore of Lake Superior to the end of the Gunflint Trail at Gull Lake. He remembers especially the extreme ranges of temperature, from -40F in the winter to 95F in the summer; the idyllic, Mediterranean days of mid-summer; the blazing, wool sweater glories of autumn and the numbing cold and heavy snows of winter. There were often straight line winds that created a matchstick tangle of forest in moments for five miles and left an acre of delicate fireweed spires blooming in the middle of the destruction.

The lake effect is still a given every winter. This strange phenomenon creates a warmer border of air from the North Shore 15 miles up the Trail to Greenwood Lake Road. This demarcation is so definite that Dell has seen years when in late March it can literally be spring on the south side of the road and still winter on the north side. "And sometimes it would be raining on one side of the road and dry on the other," he recalls.

Climatologists have determined there is a mysterious current of air flowing along the Greenwood Lake Road, close to where the Lake effect ends and "which probably has something to do with elevation gradients that create a definite border between two microclimates in the same zone," Dell says.

When Fred Dell became an observer for the Weather Bureau, he made daily trips along the Gunflint Trail and the side roads measuring temperature, precipitation and wild direction and velocity. One of his favorite winter trips was along the Greenwood Road where a mysterious current of air flows along a temperature gradient that Fred claims makes it winter on one side of the road and spring on the other.

"Another thing that has always puzzled me," Fred goes on, "is that year after year there are three places on the Trail where the snow is always deeper than anyplace else: seven miles up from town at the Pines, the Greenwood Lake Road, and Bearskin Lake. It never fails, and I don't know the answer, but this happens every year."

He has also observed many phenomena that seemingly have no explanation, such as the Northern Lights making a humming noise and that their appearance is often followed by a storm.

Dell began his weather observation activities in Fergus Falls, Minnesota in 1946, when he bought KGDE (now KBRF)—the oldest rural radio station in America still on the air (since 1922). He soon discovered he had a big competition problem. One of the strengths of the local newspaper was its weather news, which the local farmers read faithfully, instead of listening to Fred's radio station, because KGDE had no weather programming. This was before the days of the National Weather Service's electronic network and Fred knew he had to get accurate local weather information on the air for the farmers, so he began to learn all he could about weather and forecasting so he could be his own weather service.

There was a rather eccentric jeweler in town who brought the preciseness of his craft and several instruments of his own making to his hobby of weather prediction studies and he taught Dell all he knew. In a few weeks Dell was on his own because the jeweler killed his wife and was packed off to jail.

In 1961, he sold the station and moved to Minneapolis, but he had vacationed on the Gunflint Trail since boyhood and always had a strong hankering to live in the Gunflint region. So in October of 1975, he and Jenny left the cities for the Gunflint, where he bought a Voyageur's Point home on Poplar Lake and lived for 30 years.

Today there are eight volunteer weather observers in the region: four for the County Soils and Water department, which collect data for the State Climatologist; and four for the United States Weather Bureau, which needs current conditions data used in developing forecasts. Certainly this has become a much more efficient and accurately instrumented system, but I like my fantasy picture of Fred Dell snowshoeing along the Greenwood Lake Road with his ruler in one hand and a wet finger into the wind.

The islands, forests, bays, points and seemingly limitless expanses of water were all familiar sights to the Voyageurs as they paddled and portaged their way across the continent during the fur century. Saganaga, where the Gunflint Trail ends, was one of those big lakes they traversed unerringly from the Sag channel through shoreless expanses of water and hundreds of islands straight to Monument Portage and their northwest journey.

CHAPTER 8

The Voyageur's Highway:
"Thoroghfare to Empire."

—J. Wesley White

Perched next to the tarmac canoe launch at the end of the Gunflint Trail, and just before the canoeist encounters the bewildering expanse of Saganaga, is a large, rustic sign that informs visitors of the historical significance of this segment of the Voyageur's Highway—the fabled waterway that ran from La Chine, Quebec, to Great Slave Lake in Canada's Yukon Territory:

Saganaga Lake was once on the great water highway that extended 3,000 miles from Montreal to the Pacific. During the 17th, 18th and 19th centuries voyageurs in "North" canoes transported trade goods to the Indians and returned with cargoes of furs, the "gold of the northwest" for eastern markets.

These waters were extensively used by traders of the Hudson's Bay Company, the North West Company and the American Fur Company.

Across the very top of the Gunflint Trail region, like a wide, flat blossom on a gangly stem, spreads the primal beauty of the Voyageur's Highway: the 25 lakes, five rivers and over 40 portages between Lake of the Woods and Grand Portage on Lake Superior that form the international boundary between Minnesota and Ontario, the main artery of the Quetico-Superior's Boundary Waters Canoe Area Wilderness.

Robert Wheeler, in *Voices From the Rapids*, wrote, "The retreating glaciers left a watery legacy along the southern rim of the Laurentian Plateau...the Ottawa and St. Lawrence rivers, the Great Lakes and the Boundary Waters... the canoe route known to untold generations." Many readers of fur trade history are surprised to learn that this area of Minnesota was traversed by white men not long after the Pilgrims settled in the New England area.

Most of the Boundary Waters region is similar now to when it was first used. Close to a century ago it was heavily logged, but with federal protection it has now regenerated to its former glory of pristine lakes and rivers, indigenous vegetation, wildlife and the largest roadless sub-boreal forest left on the continent.

Of a similar size, the Quetico Provincial Park just over the international border forms over two million acres of visual and silent splendor, providing a quality wilderness experience for everyone to enjoy.

The Wilderness Act of 1964 described the Boundary Waters as: "an area where the earth and its community of life are untrammeled by man, where man himself is a visitor but does not remain...retaining its primeval character and influence without permanent improvements or human habitation, which is protected and managed to preserve its natural condition...affected primarily by the forces of nature, with the imprint of man's work substantially unnoticeable."

It is not precisely accurate to call it a wilderness if, by using that term, we mean a landscape undisturbed by humankind. Each year thousands of canoe parties paddle and portage its unspoiled waters, where reservations are needed long in advance if a visit is planned. Said one canoe outfitter: "It is more like a big state park." On the main routes there are sometimes several canoe parties lined up waiting to get over portages, and between Memorial Day and Labor Day the designated campsites are usually filled. But, historically and by legislative mandate, it is a wilderness, although wildness is probably a more accurate term for this enchanted landscape.

This segment of the Voyageur's Highway was almost abandoned by the fur trade after the border confusion of the Jay Treaty signing at the end of the Revolutionary War. When the French were aced out of the fur trade by the British, the Grand Portage depot was closed in 1804 in favor of Fort William on Canadian soil 30 miles up the Superior shore. The canoe brigades were then sent by the British along the old trade route up the Kaministiquia River from Fort William, Ontario, through Lac Des Mille Lacs, Pickerel and Sturgeon Lakes, over the top of Hunter's Island, down the Maligne River, then back to the boundary waters at Lac La Croix. It was a longer, harder paddle with miserable portages and the voyageurs had to be coaxed and bribed to use it, but it effectively eliminated use of most of the Pigeon River route from Grand Portage to La Croix.

The French lost control of the fur trade after only about 30 years and after that the voyageurs were really a French Canadian labor force working for the British, but the fur trade was dependent to its last breath on the canoes of the French voyageurs from hamlets such as Three Rivers, Sorel and L'Original along the Quebec shores of the St. Lawrence River. In *The Voyageurs*, Grace Lee Nute calls them "the first real explorers of the continent."

The voyageurs, colorful adventurers who manned the fur brigades, called the area *Bois Forts*, or Strong Woods. This immense forested land sweeps northwest-ward from the north shore of Lake Superior through Manitoba's Whiteshell Provincial Park, on into the prairie and tundra of the Saskatchewan River drainage, then northwest to the Great Slave country and the Mackenzie River Valley.

This Pigeon River route had not yet been discovered during the first century of the fur trade when traders and *coureurs du bois*—the illicit, freelance traders—sought the "soft gold" of the French. Previously, they traveled south and west from Michilimackinac at the confluence of Lakes Huron and Michigan, and from Detroit at the confluence of Lakes Huron and Erie, then across Wisconsin and Illinois down the Mississippi, west and north to the Platte, the Missouri and eventually the whole of the Rocky Mountain west. Fur traders and trappers were seen on the streets of New Orleans, St. Louis and Santa Fe in the 1600s, before their red-tipped paddles ever furrowed the waters of the Pigeon River route.

The 20-year-old trapper and freelance fur trader, Jacques de Noyon, was the first white man to travel the entire length of the border route by canoe from Pigeon River to Lake of the Woods in 1688. He was followed by traders De la Noue and Pachot, but this first water trail, called the Pigeon River route, from Grand Portage on Lake Superior to Lake of the Woods, was first mapped in 1731 by Pierre Gaultier de Varennes, Sieur de La Verendrye. He, with three of his four sons and a nephew, explored the region and constructed forts as far west as Rainy Lake and Lake of the Woods. One of the teenagers, Christophe Du Frost de la Jeremaye, was the first to push across the *Kitchi Onigaming*, or "great carrying place," around the nine mile cataract of the Pigeon River. La Verendrye had little interest in the fur trade beyond fulfilling some contracts he had signed to help finance his explorations. He was an explorer and his reason for travel-ing the boundary waters was to find the fabled Northwest Passage to the Orient, which he failed to do.

In spite of its relatively short life as a major fur trade route, the Minnesota seg-ment of the Voyageur's Highway played a significant role in the history of the north country and the fur trade, which was the biggest business in the world at that time. Curiously, the area owes its fur trade heritage to the fortuitous occur-rence of two tree species: the aspen, the bark of which the beavers ate; and the birch, which supplied the bark for canoes.

In addition, the trade made history aware of this curious figure, the French/Canadian voyageur, who like the cowboy of the American west, is an often misinterpreted and misportrayed hero of American history.

We are most familiar now with the voyageur image from billboards, community statues and advertisements: a tall, rangy, handsome fellow; an early Marlboro man, in fringed buckskins, canoe on his shoulders, paddle in hand, a tumplined bale of furs on his back, striding over a pine-studded portage.

History portrays him a little differently. Thomas McKinney, who traveled the country in 1826, described the voyageur as being about five feet four inches tall, usually a teenager when he entered the trade seeking adventure, and "if he shall reach five feet ten he is forever excluded from becoming a voyageur. There is no room for the legs of such people in these canoes." From paddling forty strokes a minute for sixteen hours a day and often carrying two ninety-pound pieces, or bales of fur, over rough portages, his upper body was overdeveloped with large muscular arms and shoulders, "but all looked weak in the legs and were of light weight," writes McKinney. They were old at thirty-five and few lived beyond forty-five Understandably, strangulated hernias were the usual cause of death.

The literature of fur trade history is full of descriptive passages of the voyageur. Few of them fit the image we have created for promotional purposes. Perhaps closest to our vision is Don Berry's voyageur in *A Majority of Scoundrels*, where he is portrayed as "he of the flashing paddles and endless song, the red feather in the hat, the braggadocio and the strut."

In her crackling language, Meridel Le Sueur describes the voyageur a little differently in *North Star Country*:

"They came down in the spring race of water, their narrow canoes laden with furs. They were for the most part the rag tag and bob tail of the wilderness; rascally, hiring themselves out—men who could bear the pinch of hunger like stoics and eat like hungry wolves, grumble when there was nothing to complain of, and endure the hardships of the wilderness without a murmur. They could cheat, drink, work like slaves...sing profane songs in the evening that sounded like a hundred foxes with their tails in a trap."

There was little individuality expressed in dress. The voyageur uniform was "a red woolen cap, a short shirt, cloth or deerskin trousers (or breechcloth) and moccasins," according to Grace Lee Nute. A few other items added color to his costume: he often affected a long blue capote, or cape, which was folded and used to pad the canoe thwarts during a portage, a red sash and wool cap with ostrich feathers, with a beaded bag at his waist. He would create quite stir on the Boundary Waters today, but would still be lionized because he could paddle farther, sing louder, drink more, and carry more weight over steep and rocky portages than any man before or since.

He was a bundle of paradoxes, this voyageur, forced by the economics of the fur trade to be an indentured servant. He was wild and free on the trail—vulgar but courteous, especially to the ladies and his employers. Most of the voyageurs were illiterate but clever, profane, superstitious and easily frightened but religious. They would not travel at night and were in constant fear of the Folly of the Woods, a giant beaver that stole men's minds, and the Windigo, "a horrible forest demon," which was, according to Mari Sandoz in *The Beaver Men*, "a naked, giant cannibal with a sinister, hissing cry so loud and eerie that voyageurs for whom it was intended could hear him for miles."

In addition to the Folly and the Windigo, the voyageur was afraid of the water—another paradox. He was one of the great watermen of history, traveling by canoe thousands of miles over dangerous rivers and storm-tossed lakes, but most couldn't swim and the boiling river rapids and the high waves of open water they traversed produced a dislike bordering on terror. According to some diaries, the voyageur hated the dark, brooding woods, the threatening waters, and couldn't wait to put this threatening wilderness behind him.

In fact, there is much evidence that the voyageurs didn't like it here. In *Where The Sky Began*, John Madson writes:

"The *coureurs de bois* suddenly became *coureurs de preries*, showed the joy of men suddenly emerging from darkness into light. Behind them were the ambush threatened portages of the north, and the foaming rivers where hard traveling men might lose supplies and be forced to live on stews of rock tripe and tree bark. Now they were out in the open on broad, placid rivers provided by *le bon Dieu* for a swift and direct passage."

When the voyageur quit the company after working free of his bondage, deserted to become a freelance trader or else retired, he chose more open country, and settled in areas throughout the upper Midwest that were more to his liking and where his heritage still remains: Prairie du Chein, Green Bay, and La Crosse—all in open Wisconsin countryside. Each has voyageur history. Similarly, Dubuque, Iowa, St. Louis, Missouri and St. Peter, Minnesota are all voyageur towns. But there are no such place names along the Voyageur's Highway. There is a large group of French settlements south of Winnipeg where the country suddenly opened up after winding through the trackless wilderness of the "Strong Woods" and Manitoba's Whiteshell Provincial Forest at the western end of the wooded segment of the Voyageur's Highway. Communities with names like St Genevieve, Beausejour, St. Agathe, Giroux, La Broquerie and others suggest settlement by wandering French adventurers from the fur century.

Most of these men were originally farmers and many of them returned to farming. The lure of adventure, ample brush wine, freedom and "dusky maidens" drew many of them from the farms of Quebec. Most of their ancestors were farmers from Normandy and the Loire Valley. There was no forest environment in their backgrounds. The Voyageur's Highway was a place of servitude and danger to them and they longed for the freedom of spacious, open sky country.

Other than items from the wreckage of canoes found at the base pools of some river rapids and waterfalls by Associate Director Bob Wheeler of the Minnesota Historical Society's underwater search for fur trade artifacts, there is virtually no evidence of the voyageurs ever having been here. They were here, always moving fast, for almost a century, but left no visible heritage. There is little literature and no artwork. No settlements were ever made, and none of them ever returned. Marabouef Lake near Gunflint, Lac La Croix west of Ely and the Maligne River are the only French names left along the "Strong Woods" section of the Voyageur's Highway.

There is a strong possibility there are a few living artifacts from the Voyageur days that have yet to be well researched. Canoe trippers first noticed a grove of white oak trees on Monument portage between Saganaga and Cypress Lake (Ottertrack on old maps). Later, similar groves were discovered on other portages down the border canoe route. Some are in rings which would indicate the original trees died off and the current ones are the offspring from acorns cast out from the original groves.

Oaks do not grow anywhere else in this boreal forest, so why are they on these portages? The speculation is that they were planted by the voyageurs for two reasons. One would be to make the portage easily visible and the other is more sentimental. The voyageurs were always homesick and they missed the oaks of their homeland, so they brought a few acorns with them and scattered them at portages—the only places they touched land on their journeys.

The faint melodies of paddling chansons on the drifting smoke of spirit fires, the long rippling V of a beaver's wake on a quiet pond, or these white oak groves on some portages are the only reminders left in this wild place to recall history's legacy along the Voyageur's Highway.

All travel was by canoe, that magnificently designed phenomenon of the Native Americans, which, like the snowshoe (also a Native American product), was so near perfect that neither design has changed much since its first use. It is impossible to say when the canoe was "invented." Made of completely organic material, the wood, bark and leather remains of the earliest models decomposed long ago. A good guess would probably be around 1,000 AD. It is likely that the earliest birch bark canoes were built by Algonquin tribes of the northeastern United States. Farther south and out of the canoe birch country, the hollowed log dugout served as water transportation.

The earliest activity in North American fur trading took place in the early 1500s when Montagnais from north of the St. Lawrence River paddled their big canoes out into the Atlantic to trade furs with the sailors aboard the French, Portugese, English and Basque fishing boats working the Grand Banks. Later, Algonquin and Huron canoes of furs came down the Ottawa River to the coast, and by 1580, ships were coming to shore stations from St. Malo, France, specifically for furs. The supply of beavers in this northeastern habitat was soon depleted and the fur trade moved inland by 1600.

Most of the canoes used in the fur trade, other than the small 15-footers called fishing canoes, were not built by the Native Americans, although they did build large, high-ended craft that could traverse rivers and cleave big water with heavy loads. But the trade canoes were built later by French canoe makers who learned and improved on the Native American technique. When the fur trade was at its peak, fur trading companies were ordering a dozen to as many as sixty large canoes per season, and the Native Americans had neither the production facilities nor the inclination to establish reliable canoe manufacturing yards. Their role was primarily to be suppliers of the materials used in the canoes, and later to be guides. The objects of their harvesting were primarily fifteen-foot rolls of birch bark, which were aged in the storehouse for two years then soaked well before molding to the canoe frame; lengths of northern white cedar, the primary canoe wood used for framing and ribs because of its light weight, strength and decay resistance; tamarack (larch), black spruce or black ash for thwarts and gunwales; watap, or spruce roots, for sewing and lashing; and a large supply of spruce gum, which was mixed with animal fat to keep it pliable, and used to patch and repair.

The standard of the industry, the Montreal canoe, or *canot du Maitre* (canoe of the master), which was 35 to 40 feet long, five feet wide, two and a half feet deep, was manned by sixteen paddlers and carried several tons of supplies and merchandise. This canoe was the creation of Louis le Maitre, of Three Rivers, Quebec—the master canoe builder. Le Verendrye pushed west to the Rocky Mountains in canoes from the Le Maitre yards in Three Rivers, Quebec. Three generations of Le Maitre descendants provided canoes to the fur trade.

Making canoes was a multi-generational family enterprise among the French. In addition to the LeMaitres, Auger, Littonville, Larocq, Longueil, Renard, Du Guay, Hanelle and Durant were some of the French families who maintained canoe building yards for several generations along the water route from Three Rivers, Quebec, to Grand Portage, Minnesota. Although the big canoes were sometimes used on inland waters, loads were most often transferred to the lighter, more maneuverable French-built North canoes for travel on the Voyageur's Highway. These were 25 feet long and three feet wide, thus smaller, lighter and easier to handle on portages. There was an in-between size, also used on inland lakes, called the bastard canoe, which was paddled by ten men.

There was only an interval of about 57 years between the last canoes of the fur trade using the Voyageur's Highway and the beginning of recreational canoeing. The first recorded canoe trip of this more familiar sort was the honeymoon of William and Jennie Robinson in1897, according to a document by Mrs. Robinson in the St. Louis County Historical Society in Duluth, entitled "A Honeymoon in a Birch Bark Canoe."

This incident caught the attention of forest historian, J. Wesley White, who noted that "Their trip began at Fall Lake after a three-mile carry." White assumes this meant a trip on the railroad spur from Ely to Winton on the shore of Fall Lake. In Mrs. Robinson's account of the trip, she notes, "We never saw another soul until we were within a few hours of getting back—and that single exception was a lone fisherman on Basswood Lake."

There are also records available of trips by Gen. C. C. Andrews, Minnesota's apostle of forests, taking several extended canoe trips from Winton to Grand Portage in 1901, 1905 and 1907 (at which time he was 77 years of age). White also quotes an item from the May 31,1901, *Ely Miner*, describing a canoe trip by a party of men from Duluth "whose two week route extended from Fall Lake to Gunflint. They returned by skirting the southern shores of Hunter's Island."

White continues his history of canoeing in the Boundary Waters by saying, "Perhaps wilderness canoeing was beginning to catch the popular fancy. In the fall of 1908, a Duluth newspaper carried a full page story about the canoe routes of northeastern Minnesota." Ten days later another story appeared, describing a canoe trip by the Weyerhauser and Hornsby families, a trip during which these prominent lumber families had a very narrow escape from a lightening strike.

It is also apparent that President Theodore Roosevelt began taking more interest in the Boundary Waters area of the Superior National Forest he established in 1909, as he made several canoe trips here before 1914. Three decades of century-defining events—the First World War, the Great Depression and the Second World War—followed one another distracting Americans from vacation travel, so it wasn't until 1946 that the old Voyageur's Highway once again became the wilderness destination of thousands of canoeists.

Canoes on the Voyageur's Highway today compare to the old birchbark freight canoes about like a sports car does with an SUV. Weight, size, durability and handling ease are the obvious differences as form followed function. Today's canoes are largely recreational craft and technology has changed everything but the fundamental design.

I visited with Dave Seaton, the wiry, articulate owner of Hungry Jack Canoe Outfitters near the Gunflint Trail, as he meticulously packed ten big Duluth packs with all the necessities for a canoe party's week in the wilderness. Seaton, like most canoe outfitters, is a man of many talents and abilities. Among his other winter chores he makes guitars, and is presently working on travel guitars made of native woods from trees that have blown down in the big storm for his canoe parties to take on wilderness trips.

Having owned an aluminum canoe since they came on the market 40 years ago, I was curious about the new slim, plastic canoes used by many outfitters now. New materials and some design modifications have created new canoes that are strong, easy to handle and, most important, very light and easy to portage.

Seaton gave me a quick course on the construction and use of these new canoes: "Many are Kevlar, a DuPont aramid fiber fabric used in much canoe construction now," he said. "Those fibers are actually stronger than steel. They won't tear or break and the epoxy resin adheres to Kevlar better than it does to glass, so less has to be used, making the canoe lighter. A 16-foot Souris River Kevlar canoe weighs only about 40 pounds. It's the same stuff that's used in the manufacture of sports cars.

"It flexes with the movement of the canoeist and the water. All canoe designs have specific limitations and these are not racing canoes, which are rigid, but are super tripping canoes. We have ten different kinds and sizes of canoes because we have to tailor the canoe to the canoeist's ability level and the trip. We even still have some aluminum canoes for those on a little tighter budget or for boulder bangers like you."

Before my current aluminum canoes, I had an Old Town cedar strip canvas-covered canoe with which we had to make "wet foot" landings. A few feet from shore, we stopped, stepped out into the water and lifted the canoe and its contents onto shore to keep the hull from being damaged on rough or rocky landings. Was this necessary with the new epoxy resin canoes?

"Oh yes," Seaton replied. "I think running canoes into shore is a midwestern phenomenon. We give each party a few minutes training on how to be careful canoeists and let them know what we expect from them. With these light canoes you can do the wet foot thing easily without having to lug a heavily loaded 80-pound canoe up and out of the water. Remember, a canoe must always be either completely in, or completely out, of the water to be safe from hull damage.

"Then, before the canoe party shoves off, we put three layers of duct tape along the keel line at the bow and at the stern, and if they bring the canoe back with grooves worn through the duct tape, they know we will expect them to get out their checkbook. This is usually very effective and we rarely have any serious damage done to a canoe, unless it is accidental.

"Another interesting thing we see now is a generational change in the value systems of canoeists. Many years a ago, when I started outfitting canoe trippers, we used to have to make little sweeps a few times each summer, taking big, black plastic bags out into the wilderness and bringing them back full of litter. No more. Now, just before they get their permit, we show them a video about keeping the wilderness clean and we have almost no litter problems at all."

At the height of the fur trade activity, there were probably a thousand canoes on the boundary waters each year. Today 200,000 canoeists use this superb recreational area annually. Dave Seaton breaks down canoe trippers as vacationers and adventurers. The vacationers—the largest group and about 95 percent of his business—usually take three- to five-day trips and stay within 30 miles of Hungry Jack Outfitters. The adventurers, most of whom have much of their own equipment and don't need an outfitter, go farther out into the wilderness area and stay between seven and ten days.

Canoe trippers come from a very eclectic set of backgrounds: Scout troops, honeymooners, fishermen, wilderness lovers, family vacationers, church and school groups, camp groups from mostly midwestern states where a one week canoe trip is offered as part of the camp experience, and many groups of college friends who take annual reunion canoe trips.

There was even a cross-dressing group of homosexuals from San Francisco, whom Seaton describes as "absolutely great, friendly people," who went the same route at the same time as a pair of fathers and sons from a small Iowa town. They all left the dock together and the boys were fascinated by their neighbor's hands which had different color nail polish on each finger. They camped the first night in the same general area and a couple of the boys who sneaked off to do a little spying came running back shouting, "That one guy is wearing a dress!"

"We also outfit quite a few artists and photographers who are going on image finding trips," Seaton adds. "One of the differences between this end of the Boundary Waters and the Ely end is that whereas they probably have better fishing and smaller lakes, we have larger lakes and grander scenery in this area. That comes mainly from having a greater elevation change. Thunder Point on Knife Lake over toward Ely is a beautiful high spot, but there are none of the 450-foot cliffs and hiking trails we have in this area. We outfit a lot of parties who want to hike the Border Route Trail as part of their canoe trip."

This vast expanse of the original boundary waters segment of the Voyageur's Highway still remains virtually unpopulated. "Traversed" seems to be the operative word in considering its human history. Indigenous peoples from several cultures and centuries, usually hunting or trapping parties, traversed the region. After white settlement, which was negligible, prospectors traversed it briefly and left, finding nothing of value. Large populations of beaver, pine marten, fisher, fox and timber wolf tempted trappers to traverse its more remote reaches for years. Loggers traversed it like a plague of locusts during the early century on their way west in search of more lumber to build the growing nation.

With the passing of the first Wilderness Bill in 1926, Agriculture Secretary Jardine signed a proclamation establishing 640,000 acres on the American side of the border, and Canada followed with a segment of the Quetico Provincial Park as wilderness areas with "no roads and no recreation development." Today it has been much enlarged and canoe parties, dog sled mushers, hikers, fishermen, cross country skiers and campers traverse the region, but no one stays. No one ever has. Its wild solitude is rarely disturbed for long.

Betty Hemstad

The stemless lady's slipper, or moccasin flower, is perhaps the most common member of the orchid family in northeastern Minnesota. The plant, which does not usually produce a flower for eight years will live for decades if its habitat is not disturbed.

CHAPTER 9
Gunflint Vignettes

In *Hole in the Sky*, author William Kittredge states that we must have our stories, that they are our primary connection to the landscape we inhabit.

Vignettes are the short stories of non-fiction. They can be anecdotes, legends, ornaments or memoirs. What they must be is illustrative, designed to strengthen or enlarge an impression. In the case of a Gunflint region picture, the little stories serve to intensify the color and connect us to this land.

The Bog: A Wilderness by Default

To most who enjoy the outdoors, the word "wilderness" is synonymous with an area like the million-acre Boundary Waters Canoe Area Wilderness along the northern rim of the Superior National Forest in northeastern Minnesota. It is the wild, undeveloped boreal forest, sprinkled and laced together with lakes and rivers, a much loved sanctuary away from the electronic world into forest cathedrals.

But wilderness is a word we use very carelessly. The bogs of the Gunflint region are the only true wildernesses in the area—most of them undisturbed, obscure and a little other-worldly. Not the riverine, embayment or vast peatland bogs, but the little enclosed bog, usually under ten acres of coffee-colored water, the sedgemat and stunted spruce surrounded Camelots of wilderness. Miniature kingdoms of mist, mystery and beauty.

There is nothing in the bog anyone wants: nothing to cut, mine, sell or develop so it is a wilderness by default. Bogs grow and disappear at glacial speed, tremble with mats of decomposing vegetation and sphagnum, sometimes are deep and are usually freckled with miniature forests of bog willow, tamarack, black ash, sedge grasses and stunted black spruce several hundred years old—mossy grottos of silence.

Over centuries the decaying vegetable material turns into peat, which records and preserves everything imbedded in it—seeds, pollen, insects, sometimes even human corpses. Some of the plants growing there are most often found in either the Arctic or the tropics. Tiny anomalies. In *Bogs of the Northeast*, Charles Johnson describes the bog ambience well:

'We find them intriguing, yet we shun them as somewhat peculiar," he writes. "They remain mysterious—neither solid land nor water, but a realm in between...An aura of spirits still emanates from them to stir our imaginations...While the scientist in us seeks to understand them, the poet in us wants to keep them away from complete discovery, safe in some shadow of mystery."

In the summer they are wondrous flowery realms, jewel boxes of the far north revealing bottle gentians, rosemary, bog laurel, sundews and cotton grass, the strange leathery brown blossoms of the pitcher plant, moccasin flowers, the rare rose pogonia, dragon's mouth and bog orchids. Because of the acid water and lack of food there, wild creatures usually pass through on their way to someplace else. Red-necked grebes, Lincoln's sparrows, great gray owls, common yellowthroats, sedge wrens and Connecticut warblers are the birds most often seen in bog environments. Damselflies and whirligig beetles disturb the water's surface and the rare Bog Copper butterfly is found most often in bog habitat. Frogs seem to like the bog and there is usually an abundance of chorus frogs, gray tree frogs, northern leopard frogs and wood frogs.

Occasionally a moose will frequent the shoreline area if there are aquatic vegetables like lily pads growing there. It stands near the water's edge and puts its head under water, groping with huge leathery lips to wrap around the stem of the plant near the bottom and then, with an explosion of water, jerks it out by the roots and stands for minutes leisurely chewing on the tuber the Native Americans used for years as a potato.

Many of these bogs are unmapped and deep in the woods and there are no manmade trails that lead to them because they aren't fishing spots, since the water is too acidic from the rotting vegetation for fish. This is not game animal habitat and the open water is too small to canoe, so they are virtually unknown.

The Ellefolk: A Local Legend of Norse Origin

Some bogs in this area are home to the ellefolk, the strange little people of Norse legend who are said to have emigrated here from Norway at about the same time the people of that country made new homes along the North Shore of Lake Superior and in the wooded uplands of the Gunflint region. Ellefolk lived originally in the bogs of Denmark, but they are solitude loving creatures and the almost constant ringing of the Danish church bells upset them so they finally moved to wilder, quieter places in Norway. After residing in the Norwegian bogs for years, that country too became noisy and crowded.

Norwegian immigrants who came here to fish the waters of Lake Superior wrote home about the natural beauties and remoteness of the Gunflint region of Minnesota and it wasn't long before a colony of the ellefolk decided to follow. Just how they got here is still a puzzle, but the ways of little people have always been shrouded in mystery. They can travel with great ease through air, fire, wood, water and stone. The females can even travel on moonbeams. Ellefolk are light elves associated with flowers and natural beauty, not the dark elves who will lead you astray.

The ellefolk men wear broad brimmed black hats and red sashes and are about the size of children because they only grow during moonlight hours. When they first came, many lived in the forest, but after so much of that was cut down they moved to the more secluded bogs. They usually live under the crests of small hills at the edge of the bog and they grow fabulous gardens which are hidden in the moss. They aren't seen by many people because they come out only during the hours of dawn and dusk and the males spend a lot of time sitting on the edge of the bog telling stories or playing their odd little flute-like instruments made from bog reeds and willow bark.

Some people who have poked around the bogs have fund strange, flattened sedge rings and were puzzled by them. Actually, those rings are the rings where the ellefolk dance, and if you step into one of the rings you can feel the musical vibrations of the dance. That can be dangerous because it is said you may die if you stay in the ring for too long. Many strange deaths have occurred in the bog, but it is more likely that the Norwegian legend has been misunderstood and that "transformation" is more likely what is meant. What the ellefolk legend says is that "you will never be the same."

Most dismiss the whole concept as folklore, or worse, but fortunately the Troll Lady was available to help me out as I tried to explain the ellefolk to others. In real life the Troll Lady is Norwegian born Lise Lunge-Larsen, storyteller, actress, authority on the little people of Scandinavia, and author of The Troll With no Heart in his Body.

Discussing the little people in her book, she muses. "I think they have withdrawn into an elusive world, parallel but not easily accessible to ours. In our civilized world most people have lost touch with nature and aren't capable of seeing the beings that live there. In Norway our lives were informed by stark and dramatically beautiful surroundings so I knew where the trolls lived and I knew where the wood elves would play their music."

For those who never want to lose touch with nature, it might be well to discover and adopt one of the Gunflint region's bogs. Because of its isolation and uselessness to the economy, it would always be there for you—wild, mysterious and magic.

The Lake Trout: A Gunflint Signature Specie

Several years ago I wrote a book about area wildlife and a reviewer, perhaps justifiably, chided me for being a bit elitist and only writing about "those of the fur and feather persuasion," or the more glamorous species. I ignored, she said, "the cold blooded, the photosynthetic, the slimy, the spineless" and concentrated on only those species that receive much media focus and public attention: moose, bald eagles, wolves, loons, beavers, owls and others the National Park Service refers to as the "charismatic megafauna."

Guilty, I suppose, but my self-justifying reasons for selecting these signature species are that these are the creatures that have become the emblems of North country, the stuff of legends, subjects for artists, photographers, writers, advertisers and symbol selectors of all types, to the point where the creatures have become the images by which the area is identified.

We have thousands and thousands of insects, amphibians, rodents and mollusks from the little world underfoot, but the old stories don't glorify them and somehow they don't provide the awkward majesty of a looming moose, the solemn dignity of a great gray owl, the flat out turn of a plunging lake trout, or the eerie ridge-top keening of hunting wolves. These are our flagship species, the ones people identify with and rally around.

The bay-breasted warbler perches here at the southern edge of its range anticipating outbreaks of spruce budworms; the ghostly Canada lynx, who pays close attention to the hare population, may, or may not live here; the three-toed woodpecker, a rare specie, is sometimes seen probing dead jack pines for a type of bark beetle; the Arctic snowy owl occasionally floats in on winter wings if its lemming prey of the far north becomes scarce. Goshawks, northern brook lamprey, boreal owls and several mussels are only a few of the thousands of species here that are uncelebrated but important components of the diverse wildlife population.

Many of these species exist in other areas of the state too, but I consider the symbolic Gunflint species the ones that exist primarily in this region. The lake trout (*Salvelinus namaycush*), largest of the chars, is among the oldest residents here, the First Fish, inhabiting these waters for several thousand years. Its future is not bright and biologists call it a "limited resource," but it is the most indigenous fish and first among equals. The walleye, a statewide resident, which is most popular because of its superb table qualities, is a relative newcomer.

The "laker" is a trout of many names: Mackinaw in the West, Gray trout in Canada, Togue in New England. There is a variant lake trout in Lake Superior, called the paperbelly, which is found around reefs that drop off into very deep water. Still another lake trout subspecies is the fat, deep water living Siscowet. The background color of all these fish ranges from a bluish-gray to olive green and all are covered with creamy spots. The tail is deeply forked and they are compact, heavily muscled fish. Although they are unspectacular fighters that never jump out of water, they are head-shakers and fast swimmers.

They have been known to reach one hundred pounds, but forty is tops in the sport fishery. At Gunflint Lake, where the lake trout are native, twenty pounders were quite common at one time, but that would be a rare trophy today. As fishing pressure increases, the big ones become more scarce because it takes many years to attain that size in these cold waters. It finds water above 62 degrees intolerable.

Years ago, my first fishing experience in the Boundary Waters region was a trip for lake trout. Now, a few decades later and on the same water, I continue to be fascinated by this lustrous, big- shouldered fish which knows all the secret places of the shadowy stone jungle beneath the lake's surface. With grottos and troughs over 200 feet deep, Gunflint Lake is very cold, weedless and infertile—ideal lake trout water. The slate bottom of the lake has been configured by glacial violence into cavernous trenches, long plateaus and spiny reefs that twist and dip, dropping off into inky nothingness. During the winter and after "ice out," the lake trout can be found in shallow water near shore, but by July the surface layers of the lake have warmed enough to send them down below the thermocline into water that stays in the low 40s, which is usually 65 to 85 feet down.

That first lake trout trip of mine took place during the1960s when the Cold War was heating up and international fuses were getting pretty short. One rainy July day, I was out trolling for trout along the palisades on the Canadian side of Gunflint Lake with a sometimes friend. We usually argued a lot and couldn't agree on much except lake trout fishing. We were catching an occasional trout and having a good time in spite of his contrariness when it occurred to me that fishing together always seemed to patch up our usually frayed relationship. There is something about fishing that seems to melt away the prickly edges of personalities, and two people who normally don't get along very well can usually forget about their differences in a boat enjoying the magic of a fishing morning. Why, I wondered, couldn't this kind of renewal work on the international level in the quest for peace in those Cold War times?

Later that day, flushed with the brilliance of my idea, I drafted a letter to the chairman of the Olympic Committee suggesting an event which would bring together a team of Russian fishermen who pursued the Taimen *(Hucho taimen),* a lake trout cousin that swam in Russian waters, and a team of our best lake trout fishermen from Minnesota. What a great way, I figured, to promote amity and concord in spite of political differences.

The committee chairman, a crusty old gentleman named Avery Brundage, took little time answering my proposal. He came down pretty hard on the idea, and on me as well, suggesting the whole scheme was preposterous and implying that anyone who would conceive of such a plan was probably a few inches off the ground. Strangely, an event takes place now on Gunflint and nearby lakes every other year that bears a distinct resemblance to that failed project. That event began several years ago when Dr. Ron Caple, a University of Minnesota Duluth chemistry professor and virtuoso lake trout fisherman, was finishing his Gunflint Lake cabin between trips to his favorite lake trout spots.

A colleague had told Caple about a brilliant Russian chemist named William Smit, whose research into organic synthesis paralleled work Caple was doing. They corresponded and met in Russia the following year. A few moments into that meeting they discovered they were both avid lake trout fishermen. Smit came to UMD at Caple's invitation the following academic year and in their spare time away from the chemistry lab, they headed for the lake trout haunts of Gunflint and North Lakes.

Their organic synthesis work, which has many applications in medicine and agriculture, came to the attention of both the Soviet and the U.S. Academies of Science, and soon an ongoing program was set up with groups of chemists shuttling back and forth between the two countries. Caple and Smit, who is now also a UMD faculty member, have spent many summers fishing lake trout in the Gunflint area and a variety of Russian waters with the teachers and students participating in the research exchange program. Caple, who has since been elected to the Russian Academy of Science, has packed his books and fishing tackle for trips to Russia sixteen times, where he has spent his spare time fishing Lake Onega, the Shoyu River in Karelia, the Ob River in central Siberia, and other Russian trout water with his hosts. The Russian "team" of students and teachers has fished Gunflint and North Lakes with Caple and Smit

110

for as many years. In l980, when the U.S. withdrew from the Olympic games because of the Russian invasion of Afghanistan, the fishing chemists held their own competition on the Ob River in Russia and fished to a 20 to 20 tie.

When the Russian fishermen first came to Gunflint, there was a definite culture shock among both groups when it was discovered that sport fishing was not a part of the Russian background. In Russia, people fished to eat, and there was little emphasis on conservation, especially possession limits and licensing.

One day a group of Russians was playing cards on Caple's dock and watching a set line that was soaking a fat cisco in a deep hole near shore where researcher Irina Smoliakova had taken a lunker trout the year before. Around noon a Minnesota DNR boat came nosing slowly down the shore and stopped at Caple's dock. It was a conservation officer making his rounds and checking fishing licenses. Stepping out onto the dock he was greeted by toasts and good wishes in a friendly Russian chorus. Baffled, but determined, he made every effort to make himself understood, but met only more Russian salutes, handshakes, vodka toasts and lunch invitations. Seeing what was gong on, Caple hid up in the cabin peeking out the porch screen. Frustrated, but filled with the warmth of their welcome, the conservation officer finally wished them a good day and pushed off.

A trout in the landing net was the signal for everyone to head for the cabin kitchen and begin the preparation of Ucha, a delicious Russian fish soup. Caple showed them how to fillet a fish neatly and cut the fillets into bite sized pieces. They were very impressed with his demonstration, then gathered up the head, tail, skin and guts from the cleaning board and threw them all into the soup pot. Caple learned that in preparing real Ucha, the whole fish is used.

Orchid Time

Spring comes to the Gunflint Region in a laggardly way, much like a schoolboy off to his piano lesson—slowly, hesitantly, easily distracted.

First comes a false spring. Crow Winter, the natives call it. One day there will be a glimmer of hope when icicles begin to drip. Red squirrels joyfully discover hidden caches of pine nuts, but then near sunset the temperature drops, snow-stuffed clouds roll in and by morning it is winter again.

Finally there comes the softer, shining air, more velvety, that moves down the south ridge, melting snow and stirring cedar sprays. This is when the buttery, sunlight yellow of marsh marigolds are found blooming in the muck banks of opening streams, when wild music is flung down from skies by waves of migrating geese, and loons drop into the first pools of open water along the lake shore. In a few weeks it will be orchid time, a phenomenon that accents the uniqueness of this boreal forest.

The first flowers to appear—the glories of true spring—are the tiny, shade-intolerant, white flowers that carpet the forest floor. These blossom shortly after the snow melts back from the lower, thinner woods close to the lake, but before the leaves come out on the trees and understory brush. There are Canada mayflower, or false lily of the valley; bunchberry, star flower, goldthread, anemone, false Solomon's seal, and white violet. When the tree and understory leaves begin to emerge and their shadows dapple the forest floor, the pale pinks and yellows of more shade-tolerant species begin to appear: twinflowers, clintonia, pyrola and nodding trilliums.

When the wakening spring goes on into late May and early June, lake trout splash along cedar-lined shores gorging on insects falling from the trees and a phenomenon of the boreal forest bursts forth. This is orchid time.

Although orchids are perceived as a more tropical flower, there are twenty-one species of orchids growing in the spring woods and bogs of the Gunflint region. To further overcome the tropical stereotype, Welby Smith, botanist for the DNR's Natural Heritage Program and Coordinator of the Endangered Species Program, explains in *Orchids of Minnesota*, that orchids "constitute one of the largest plant families with 725 genera and an estimated 23,000 species," and that "orchids grow from the tundra to Tierra del Fuego." There are even orchids that are circumpolar in distribution. One of them that grows in northeastern Minnesota, the small northern bog orchid, has expanded its range as far north as the Arctic.

Because this area was under glaciers until about 12,000 years ago, all of the orchid species here migrated after the ice had retreated and 42 species made that trip.

"This is a rowdy, pioneering bunch of orchids," Smith says. "They could be called the advance guard, or lunatic fringe, of orchid evolution."

Comparatively few of the orchids in the tropics are ever seen because they are epiphytic—that is, they grow non-parasitically on trees, high in the canopy of tropical jungles, getting all their nutrients from the air and water. About 80 percent of the world's orchids grow like this, practically unseen, in tropical climates. The feature that makes temperate zone orchids found in the Gunflint region so attractive is their accessibility. They are terrestrial and grow on the ground at ankle to knee height where they can be examined closely.

Because of their exotic beauty, orchids are the flowers of mystery, love and sexuality. In *The Orchid Thief*, Susan Orlean tells us that "in England, Victorian ladies were forbidden from raising orchids because their flowers were too sexually suggestive for their shy constitutions."

One of the reasons we bought our Gunflint cabin 25 years ago was a discovery we made while exploring the property. A small patch of calypso orchids grew in a coronet just beneath a bedroom window. I was astonished to find these delicate flowers growing in this austere, rocky setting. The meager soil they were clinging to was mostly decomposing forest duff, some glacial till and small gravel. We bought the cabin the next day. Sometimes it is best to listen to the heart in these matters.

For several years these little fairyslippers bloomed in the late spring and I would lie on the ground and watch the little gossamer stems uncurl from a sheath in the single basal leaf and their velvety blossoms emerge from royal purple bracts, which held tight until just the right moment. According to legend, the flower would bloom only when the fairies sang. The inflated slippers with their faint purple striping and reddish spots inside were covered on top by a furry gold coverlet, yielding a complex and startlingly beautiful blossom—the ultimate gift of a Gunflint spring.

Field guides are an essential part of the orchid hunter's kit and *Minnesota Orchids*, by Welby Smith, is the best total information book available. But I am never without Alice Lounseberry's century-old *Guide to the Wildflowers*, too. It contains the required data on size, habitat, color, and range, but it seems to have been written on the spot and notes made immediately upon discovery of the flower. Lounseberry often seems overcome by the flower's revelations. Her lyrical paragraph on the calypso orchid is delightful, if not very scientific:

"It is just when we least to expect to find this lovely flower that some silken thread will probably guide us to its hiding place deep down in some mossy bog. It is very shy, tremulous and having feasted our eyes upon it we would fain creep away as softly as we came."

We have several other orchid species growing nearby, all in slightly different habitats. The rarest—the prize of the orchid hunter—is the pale pink ramshead orchid, the smallest of the ladyslippers, which has a pouch (shaped like a ram's head) traced by a web of purple veins. It prefers the acid soil of boggy places or the needle strewn carpeting found near red or white pine stands. A few have been found in the jack pine groves around Seagull Lake.

It is strange that one of the most beautiful of the temperate zone orchids has the most hideous name: the dragon's mouth. Found in grassy coniferous swamps of all types, the dragon's mouth orchid is conspicuous and easily identifiable by its large, terminal, purple to pink blossom. It is one of the orchids that doesn't seem to need soil to root as it is sometimes found on floating sedge mats with its roots in the water.

The orchid found most frequently in the Boundary Waters area is Hooker's Orchid, which usually has a couple dozen yellow blossoms on a heavy stalk, and whose largish leaves lie flat on the ground. It requires a drier soil than most orchids and so is found mostly in bedrock country and on dry jackpine ridges.

The heart-leafed twayblade is an unusual orchid in several ways. It is found frequently in northeastern Minnesota both in bogs and in upland forests. According to Smith in *Minnesota's Orchids*, it is one of the most wide ranging of all orchid plants. It has heart-shaped leaves midway on the stem and tiny, stem-clinging blossoms that can be either red, purple or green.

A pinkish-purple, bearded orchid on a slender two-foot stalk, the rose pogonia is found most often in boggy places and has a beautiful, fringed and spotted protruding lip, often used as a landing pad for the bumblebees which frequent this lightly scented beauty. It is sometimes found in the northern part of the Gunflint region, but more often in the greenstone country near Ely.

While there are other beautiful orchids in these woods—the stately, three-foot green orchid; the diminutive purple-fringed orchid; and the tall, white bog orchid whose blossoms are faintly luminescent and give it the name "bog candle"—there also grow some not-so-beautiful orchids. The tessellated rattlesnake plantain, smallest of the family, grows often at the foot of the big pines or near root throws. It clenches a tiny fist of minute white blossoms on a spike-like, downy stem no more than a few inches high. It wouldn't warrant a second look if it weren't for the rosette of basal, spade-shaped leaves with the striking white diamond streaks of a rattler.

The spotted coralroot is a fleshy plant that grows on decaying organic material. It has no leaf stem, just 20 to 30 small homely blossoms which are freckled with red spots that cling tightly to a pale pink stalk. It is fetid looking and disproportionate with the look of death about it, like the fungi it grows on.

Finally, the moccasin flower, or stemless lady slipper, has a deep pink blossom veined with crimson which gives it a look of being engorged with blood. It is the most common orchid in this region and one which grows in almost any habitat, even on rock shelves. According to Welby Smith, ideal moccasin flower habitat would consist of a mossy mat in a coniferous swamp under white cedar branches. The moccasin flower is sometimes confused with the showy, or pink and white, ladyslipper, Minnesota's state flower, which is not found in this habitat. The moccasin flower has a smallish structure, but the showy, which is in decline because of the illicit orchid trade, can grow to a height of three feet and prefers a more alkaline soil as is found in oak woods or along stone walls. The plant can live more than one hundred years, whereas few moccasin flower plants live over ten years.

The beauty of these orchids and their unexpected presence here add an aura of surprise and mystery that softens this rugged landscape and make their late spring settings holy places.

The Outlaw Bridge

The eastern edge of Gunflint country is defined by the international border that follows the wanderings of the Pigeon River as it alternately slides and tumbles through meadows, forests and over the nine-mile portage through the Grand Portage Ojibwe Reservation. It is a scuffling, wild river there, dropping 600 feet in 26 miles. Its grand exit at the High Falls, the highest waterfall in Minnesota, from the rocky cliff country paralleling the Big Lake into the flat, pre-Lake Superior lip, is a berserk, braided cascade of foam. It pours over massive black diabase dikes, 100 feet down into a spray pool of rocks and rainbows. The river is unrestrained by dams or barriers anywhere in its wild country dash from South Fowl Lake to Lake Superior. An appropriate river for an Outlaw Bridge.

Prior to 1917 there was no highway along the North Shore to a bridge crossing the Pigeon River into Ontario from Minnesota, despite the petitions of business interests of both countries. Canada did not achieve full Dominion status until 1931 and America was pre-occupied with World War I, so efforts of businessmen on both sides of the border lobbying for a new road and an international bridge were largely ignored. Consequently, a private enterprise, or "outlaw" bridge was built by impatient local businessmen of both countries eager to cash in on the rapidly growing tourist industry.

Business travel was increasing, too. The Model T Ford had opened up the area to sportsmen and vacationers. Freight hauling and bus service to areas unserved by railroads was booming, but all travelers that crossed into Canada had to go by the thrice-weekly steamship from either Duluth or Grand Marais to the

Canadian Lakehead cities of Port Arthur and Fort William, or drive over the ice along shore in the winter. The potential for commerce and the frustrations with government inaction became so strong that the Rotary Clubs of Port Arthur and Duluth and the Automobile Club of Duluth decided to organize their forces and build their own bridge and highway.

The segment of road between Mineral Center and the Outlaw Bridge at the Pigeon River was part of the Black and White Highway from Kansas City to Thunder Bay. It was also probably the worst road in Minnesota. One reporter described it as "like riding on pine logs...in fact, it was pine logs."

To hell with the governments, they said. We'll do it ourselves. And they did. Because there were no treaties, sanctions or financial support, folks called it the Outlaw Bridge and it served as the only crossing between northeastern Minnesota and Canada from 1917 to 1934 when a new steel bridge was built and officially adopted by both commonwealths. Thousands used the Outlaw Bridge, but only one car went through the wooden trusses and into the river gorge. It wasn't until 1963 that the new U.S. Highway 61, or North Shore Drive, was built in its present configuration through the Grand Portage Ojibwe Reservation and National Monument, and a new international bridge was built over the Pigeon.

Although the heyday of logging was done by the beginning of the first World War, there was still much logging in the rocky and remote parts of the Gunflint region and in northwestern Ontario.

William Scott, a Thunder Bay lumber baron, originally from Wisconsin, owned the Pigeon River Lumber Company of Port Arthur and was a founding member of the Port Arthur Rotary Club, which he inspired to sponsor the bridge. According to the *Thunder Bay Green Mantle*, he had "access to money, local government support, business interests and a lot of good timber." He also had a primitive logging road into a site on the Ontario side of the river which was ideal for a bridge: an even-sided fifty-foot chasm, which would allow a large log raft to pass under during the spring runoff without taking the bridge out. Scott used his money, influence and enormous energy to drum up support, labor and materials on both sides of the border to make the bridge and its connecting "highways" a reality.

The one lane road on the Canadian side was bad, but the one on the American side was awful. A reporter who covered the festivities during the opening of the bridge described it as "like riding over pine logs...in fact, it was pine logs." For a distance of several miles, wooden troughs had been built for the wheels to run in. Being wider, buses and trucks had to take their chances on the shoulder.

In those days, Lake Superior's North Shore Drive was quite primitive. Highway 61 was a gravel road that turned inland just north of the Reservation River (now County 17) and went to Mineral Center, a forlorn little community of dirt poor farmers that disappeared completely by 1928. It would seem from the rather grandiose name that the founders of this town had great hopes for the mining potential of the area, but like all glittering dreams of mineral fortunes in Cook County, Mineral Center tanked early. The Grand Portage Band of Ojibwe received a Congressional appropriation in the 1930s to buy back the land and include it in their reservation.

The road from Mineral Center to the Pigeon River was to become the final segment of the Black and White Highway that ran from Kansas City to Port Arthur, Ontario, crossing the Pigeon over the Outlaw Bridge.

Scott contributed all the bridge lumber, had the trusses built in Port Arthur and hauled to the site where construction began in the winter of 1916. The big spans were prefabricated in Duluth and hauled to the river by horse sleigh. The trip took a week and the men who made the trip stayed in farmhouses along the way at night.

Scott recruited hundreds of eager volunteer laborers from the Rotary Clubs of both cities, the Duluth Automobile Club, the Cook County Highway engineer, and business people from both sides of the border who would benefit from the increased traffic. The total cost was $4,801.70.

The Grand Opening, on August 18, 1917, was a gala international occasion featuring a bagpipe band, an honor guard of Canadian Mounties and a 250-member delegation of dignitaries from both countries. In the center of the bridge, lavishly decorated with flags and buntings, was a huge sign reading, "Pigeon River International Bridge of the Scott Highway. Erected by the Rotary Club." The first car across the bridge was a Winger and Robertson Ford driven by Emil Hall. In the good-feelings spirit of the occasion, officials had invited the Hon. G. H. Ferguson, Ontario Minister of Highways, who reciprocated by agreeing to pay the outstanding balance on the bridge of $768 even though his department had no record of the bridge's existence.

In spite of the poor road, the wooden bridge and the deserted wilderness around it, the bridge site grew into a bustling and elegant tourist community.

On the Canadian side, Max Hurtig built the Pigeon River Resort Hotel, which contained a large dining room, a gift shop, the post office and bar. For 40 years it remained open year-round never once closing its doors. It had eight cottages in the pines, which were very popular. Babe Ruth stayed in one during a fishing vacation and "Rudolph Valentino, heart throb of the silver screen, once checked in to the honeymoon cabin with an assumed name and an assumed sweetheart," according to Jen Thompson, writing in the April '97 issue of the *Green Mantle.* Thompson continues:

"There is still a line of jackpines, seventy years tall, behind the concrete tank where the hotel must have stood. The wild raspberries have reclaimed any evidence of the cabins which were behind the hotel. You can still glimpse the sequined river from the cliffs and imagine what a romantic place this must have been....From the end of the roadway the cliff drops 50 feet to a sparkling, serpentine river. You can watch it snake around the boulders all the way to the silver shore of Lake Superior."

She continues her reminiscence by recalling a long-standing tradition that ended with the destruction of the bridge in 1963:

"Gone were the parties Max Hurtig liked to organize every year for patrons and friends between July 1st and the 4th. 'Hands Across the Border Parties,' he called them. He would invite the Pipers down from the Lakehead for the parade and brass bands would travel up from Duluth. Mayors and dignitaries from both sides of the border would walk out onto the bridge and shake hands in the middle to exchange Canada Day and Independence Day greetings."

About the same time Hurtig built his Canadian hotel, a little resort community on the American side sprang up. It was called Sextus City after its founder and promoter, Sextus Lindahl. Old-timers remember him referred to as Senator Lindahl, but the Minnesota Legislative Library shows no such legislator ever having served. The title was apocryphal, sort of like a Kentucky Colonel, but Sextus City was very real.

Lindahl had bought up Native American allotments around the American side of the bridge and began with just a couple gas pumps, but soon had a hotel with a post office, restaurant and beer garden, filling station and 22 guest cabins. The customs and immigration office was in a tent across the road.

Bus service ran regularly up the North Shore, but they contrived to always arrive at the border after 8 p.m. when the bridge closed, so passengers were compelled to rent a room or cabin for the night. In the morning, they would walk across the bridge and get on a Canadian bus to complete their trip to Port Arthur or Fort William.

From 1920 to 1933 was the Prohibition era in the United States, but not Canada, so this remote, unofficial border crossing deep in the forest became quite a lively spot. There was much smuggling of illegal booze, and guests of the hotel and cabins in Sextus City would walk across the bridge, drink in Canada, and then wander back to their accommodations on the American side.

In 1947, the property on the American side was bought by Edward and Mabel Ryden, of Hill City, Minnesota, who added substantially to the complex. Their lodge burned to the ground in 1958, but they rebuilt and operated the business until 1963 when the new international bridge was built six miles downriver and the Ryden family moved with it, opening the historic Ryden's Duty Free Store, restaurant, filling station and motel, which is still a North Shore fixture.

Even though the bridge and the resort are gone now, a few northern European illegal immigrants have tried to cross into the U.S. at that part of the river, and occasionally drug smugglers will shoot bags of marijuana over the river border with bows and arrows. But generally it is a very scenic and peaceful area of a beautiful primeval forest incised by the rugged river canyon. A few vacation homes have sprung up, occasionally hikers from the Grand Portage Trail will pass by, as well as the occasional fisherman, members of the Grand Portage Band of Ojibwe, who are the "new" owners of the property, and sightseers who want to experience the yesterdays of the Outlaw Bridge.

John Henricksson

The peace and wilderness beauty of the Gunflint region attracts visitors from all over the world to experience what author Paul Gruchow calls "the grace of the wild."

CHAPTER 10

A Quality Wilderness Experience: More Than Just Fishing

For most of its 80 years as a recreation destination, the Gunflint region appealed mainly to fishermen, but fish are no longer as easy to come by as they were in the old days. The "old days" would be the 1920s when Russell Blankenburg sold his Wisconsin resort, Lighthouse Lodge, near Eagle River, and re-established his resort business on Lake Saganaga at the end of the Gunflint Trail because his Wisconsin guests were canceling their reservations to fish this new region they had all heard about. Great catches of walleyes, lake trout, smallmouth bass and northern pike fueled the enthusiasm of sportsmen from all over the nation, and resort cabins with two rooms and a path were springing up on many lakes accessible by road or boat throughout the region.

The fisheries resource held up remarkably well for several decades but then diminished gradually from excellent to just good, but even today fishing continues to be a big attraction. Fishing trips were most often guy things then, but by the sixties and seventies family vacations were becoming popular and when the Boundary Waters Canoe Area Wilderness became a legal entity, the business community in Grand Marais, Gunflint resorters and canoe outfitters wisely began selling "a quality wilderness experience," rather than just fishing.

The evolution of saleable recreational activities in this area faced much different challenges than most other tourist attraction areas. To encourage tourism here required considerable creativity, because most of the land here is public, under the management of the U.S. Forest Service and off-limits to most traditional development. There would be no golf courses cut into the public forest, water slides on the rivers, billboards or resort complexes with pools and casinos—none of the highly commercial but environmentally insensitive facilities that are features of many tourist areas.

As a result, the environment itself has become the attraction. The hundreds of lakes and rivers, the ice-scoured and abraded landscape, the wildlife, the rock-strewn and craggy allure of Lake Superior's North Shore, the benign beauty of the forest mosaic all have created a focus for non-consumptive recreational activities. Hiking, birding, moose watching, canoeing, camping, berry picking, biking, cross country skiing, snowshoeing, dog sledding—all these things have become the nucleus of vacation travel in the Gunflint region.

Hiking, one of the most popular activities, is outstanding as a result of the 200 miles of partnered trails in the Gunflint district where the ownership and main-tenance of the trails is shared among the U.S. Forest Service, the Minnesota DNR, private land owners, the county and volunteer organizations such as the Lake Superior Hiking Trail Association, the Kekekabic Trail Association, the Minnesota Rovers and the North Superior Ski and Run Club, which takes responsibility for the fifteen-mile Pincushion Mountain trail complex near town.

These long trails include the picturesque path along the boundary waters on the Kekekabic, the 40-mile wilderness hike between the Gunflint Trail and Ely, and the 70-mile Border Route Trail between the Grand Portage and Gunflint Lake which follows the highest elevations along the Voyageurs' Highway. The Superior Hiking Trail, a 200-mile footpath along the ridgeline from Duluth to the international border at Pigeon River, has its most beautiful 90 miles in the Gunflint region, including the spectacular chasm of the Devil Track River Gorge and the high shelf rock overlooks of Lake Superior.

The 32 shorter trails—those from one to ten miles long—are used primarily by day hikers, and have specific destinations, such as Caribou Falls, Sweetheart's Bluff, South Lake or Eagle Mountain. 142 miles of them in all. Some of these are also used by mountain bikers who have 282 miles of rugged terrain to explore.

"Mooseing," or moosewatching, is unique in this area of the eastern half of the Superior National Forest, which has been managed for moose for several years. Populations fluctuate with disease outbreaks, hunting success and the border wanderings, but there are usually about one thousand moose in this area, and they are fascinating creatures to watch.

"Wow, I had no idea they were so big," is the reaction of most first time moose watchers. They usually think a moose might be like a big deer. A big white-tailed deer may be 150 pounds, but that would be a runty moose calf and it could run right under the belly of a full grown moose, which can weigh a thou-sand pounds and stand eight feet high at the shoulder.

When the camera clicks, young Mr. Moose jerks his head out of the water and stares at the photographer who disturbed his lunch. The moose, often seen feeding in the swampy ponds next to the Gunflint Trail, seldom bolt or display much concern over people being nearby. They are one of the area's biggest tourist attractions.

Most mooseing is done from cars slowly cruising the Gunflint Trail or along the many county and forest roads. In the winter, moose can be seen on almost any icy road where the county crews spread a salt mixture. The moose drop down on their front knees to lick the salt from the road because their legs are too long to comfortably lower their heads to road level.

Moose calves are born from mid-May to early June, so the summer is a good time to see the family together. One of our best sightings was along the Seagull Creek area of the Gunflint Trail where we watched a mother moose nursing her twin calves while browsing the willow shoots next to the road. Moose are seen most often in summer either crossing the roads or feeding on aquatic vegetation in the small ponds or swamps next to the roads. Usually early morning or around dusk is the best time for moose viewing.

Fall is crazy time for the bull moose, which are almost always in a terrible temper during the rut. They attack stumps and trees, bellow constantly, pee all over everything, challenge cars and trucks on the road and are generally very anti-social. Fall is the only time of year the moose can be dangerous to man.

Coming down off the South Rim Trail one October day, we rounded a bend and came face to face with an angry bull moose standing splay-legged in the middle of the trail, his rack lowered and his eyes blazing. We remained completely still, mostly from fear, but I did remember to look off into the woods, occasionally glancing sideways at the moose. Old-timers always say, "Never stare a wild creature in the eye. It intimidates them." After a few minutes of this rapid eye movement, the bull decided we weren't much of a problem for him, so he lumbered past us as we ducked into the brush.

Moose are ideal creatures to watch because they never seem to be nervous. They don't bolt and race off like a deer. They almost seem to enjoy their stardom. A moose feeding in a swamp near the road usually occasions a line of cars parked on the shoulder with people out photographing the moose or pointing it out to their children. The moose watches the people, flaps its huge ears, goes back to feeding and eventually wanders off.

But there's more to watch on the Gunflint than moose. One of the fastest growing of these non-consumptive sports is birding, or birdwatching. It has been a passion of some birders in the Gunflint region for 75 years, but only in the past twenty years has birding broadened its appeal to most vacationers. It is a laid-back activity. In *Return of the Ospreys*, author and consummate birder, David Gessner, recognizes his own goal-oriented nature and says, "Though I want to slow down, I'm not quite ready to sink into the dirt. If I don't believe that I've managed to live completely on osprey time, I do believe that being with the birds and watching their lives has made a difference...I've become a little more patient, and I'm beginning to understand what patience is."

Birding has reached huge numbers in America. From the *Audubon Agenda* comes this startling information: "The quiet, teeming world of bird watchers and feeders now includes one-fifth of the American population, more than 50 million people (2 million in Minnesota), who outnumber hunters and fishermen combined." This makes birders potentially the largest and most powerful environmental force in the United States, and an economic gold mine.

Because of the variety and quality of habitats, the Superior National Forest has been recognized as having the greatest number of breeding bird species of any national forest, and it has been designated one of the one hundred Globally Important Bird Areas. Researchers have set up 154 forty-acre monitoring plots in the forest.

Probably the first list of Minnesota birds was loosely assembled by Jonathan Carver, an 18th century Minnesota explorer. Unfortunately the list isn't of much use to science history scholars today because it carries descriptions of such fanciful birds as the "Wakon, an unidentified, fabulous bird superstitiously venerated by the Sioux."

The year 1874 seems to be the first landmark date in Minnesota birding history. In that year the keeping of records and the beginnings of collections were started in the new Minnesota Museum of Natural History in St. Paul. Dr. Philo Hatch, a homeopathic physician from St. Anthony, was appointed State Ornithologist in that year. He seems to have been named to the post largely on the strength of his bird list: 226 species complete with notes on each bird. His list was printed in the bulletin of the Minnesota Academy of Natural Sciences, of which he was also president, and he is now considered the Father of Birding in Minnesota.

In *Audubon Art*, author Frank Graham refers to a Minnesota chapter of the National Audubon Society in 1895. At that time, bird watching was mostly a pastime of refined ladies, who were the first to protest the wanton slaughter of birds in this country by market hunters for the millinery trade, especially in Florida where the snowy egrets were rapidly being hunted to extinction. In writer Val Cunningham's fascinating account, *Birding 100 Years Ago*, there was a group in St. Paul's Merriam Park district called The Distaff Naturalist's Club of Female Bird Enthusiasts who, when confronted with the slaughter of birds for decorative feathers, could get pretty feisty.

"Johanna's mother (Mrs. Ramaley), held an afternoon tea yesterday. Each and every carriage disgorged a woman wearing a hat adorned with plumes, and in some cases, bird wings and even heads! We had made small signs advising the women to use fabric not feathers, and each of us also wore a black armband as we stood at the gate to await Mrs. Ramaley's guests. The women were terribly affronted. Mrs. Ramaley was in a great outrage and contacted each of our parents who are now debating the fate of our confederation."

The wanton destruction of birds had become a nationwide problem, and Cunningham also relates the story of ornithologist, Ludlow Griscombe, taking afternoon bird walks down Fifth Avenue in New York counting what he called "hat birds," or bird parts adorning women's hats. He averaged forty species a day including woodpeckers, warblers and owls—probably as good a list as he might have gotten on a more orthodox bird walk.

Artists, ornithologists and other scientists killed birds for purposes of identification. They called it "collecting." In a journal entry, the Minnesota birder's icon, Dr. Thomas Sadler Roberts, author of *Bird Portraits in Color* and the two volume study, *Birds of Minnesota*, tells of going to Lake Harriet in Minneapolis and killing many American mergansers for study purposes.

In response to my query about the history of bird protection, Cunningham responded, "In 1896, a group of Boston women formed the Massachusetts Audubon Society, with particular focus on stopping the millinery trade in bird feathers and plumes. In 1900, Congress passed the Lacey Act which forbade interstate trade in birds protected by any state. Yet in 1908, feathers were still being sold by the ton. Around 1912, states began passing protection laws, but national laws weren't passed until later."

By 1913 the outcry became so loud that legislation began to pass through Congress protecting passerines, or perching birds and other plumage-bearing species. According to Cunningham, those early years were the worst of times for the birds and, in spite of some habitat destruction, these are the best of times.

There isn't much evidence of birding in the Gunflint region until around 1937 when the Christian Brothers, Hubert, Pius and Leo, came to Loon Lake to inventory the birds of the upper Trail. The leader, Brother Hubert, was a naturalist and teacher at Cretin High School in St. Paul and later at St. Mary's College in Winona. He was an inveterate birder, and contributed many articles and his bird lists to *The Flicker*, now renamed *The Loon*, magazine of the Minnesota Ornithologist's Union.

In 1936, Dr. Roberts wrote "North of Lake Superior to the Canadian boundary, in Cook County, the country is rough and may almost be called mountainous...In the forests numerous northern nesting warblers and sparrows including evening grosbeaks and crossbills make their homes. It is here that spruce grouse, ravens and moose are making their last stand." Well, not really. That has not happened. It is now seventy years later and they are all still here. They, and many more birds that were part of those early birder's lists. But they started something, those early ones: Dr. Roberts, Brothers Hubert, Pius, Leo at Loon Lake, and Clair Rollings, who was working at the Gunflint CCC Camp in1939 and wrote the first detailed observations of the spruce grouse.

There are many organized birding tours of the Gunflint region now. The Victor Emanuel and the Wings tours have been annual events for 20 years. The smaller, but more frequent Minnesota Ornithologist's Union trips, are for more serious birders and use vehicles which are electronically linked so the occupants can immediately share each others' sightings. Then there are the more social outings like the Muffin Tour, guided by Duluth naturalist Kim Eckert, who has done many years of boreal owl research in the Superior National Forest. The

Muffin Tour offers an eclectic birding experience as well as a bakery and pastry munching adventure.

Celebrating the annual arrival of 155 nesting species in the Gunflint woods, including the golden-winged, black-throated blue, Canada, magnolia, chestnut-sided warblers and other marvels of the bird world, the annual Gunflint Trail Boreal Birding Days, sponsored by the Gunflint Trail Association, has taken place every year in early June. The full weekend includes six guided trips of a half day each and a special introductory course for beginning birders offered by Molly Hoffman, who has been in charge of the Audubon Christmas Bird Count for many years. In addition, she hosts a public radio bird show, contributes articles to several publications, and leads a sound identification tour called "A Bird in Your Ear."

"Many of these spring migrants are tiny birds that stay inconspicuous in the tall trees," Molly says. "If you can identify them by their songs, birding is a lot easier and more enjoyable."

The designated birding areas for the weekend are: the Lima Mountain Road, which features some of the more rare species such as the spruce grouse, the black-backed woodpecker, the solitary sandpiper and the great gray owl; the North Shore Hardwood Forest, a select habitat for the broad-winged hawk, the scarlet tanager, the wood thrush, merlins, warblers, peewees, veerys and many other birds of the hardwood forest; the End of the Gunflint Trail, where the Arctic hints of the boreal forest support observable populations of gray jays, black-backed woodpeckers, boreal chickadees and winter wrens; and the Kekekabik-Magnetic Rock and Gunflint High Cliffs Trails, a mosaic of several different niches and communities along the upper Trail where a variety of bird species find ample food, nest sites and cover. An added attraction to these trail trips are the accompanying information sessions on forest ecology and wildflower identification.

The loons, wood peewees and crows are the first ones greeting the sunrise around our cabin. We rise on the first morning of Boreal Birding Days and after drinking some coffee, and gathering notebooks, field guides, rain gear, field glasses and mosquito dope, we're ready for the rendezvous at Trail Center.

After a short van ride, we see birders strung out all along the Little Ollie Road west of the Gunflint Trail. Our guide, Dave Benson, naturalist at Hawk Ridge Nature Center in Duluth, spots a red-tailed hawk hovering over a clear-cut near the North Brule River and went into his dying mouse routine. 'Squeeeeet, oot, oot, squeeeeet," he shrills. The red tail peered back under his wing at this strange performance, hesitates and then flies on about his business.

Soon Dave locates pert little alder flycatchers, red-eyed vireos, an olive-backed thrush, a pair of winter wrens, the orange and black lightning flashes of male Blackburnian warblers, some buzzing parula warblers and a golden-crowned kinglet. As a finale to this hike we are thrilled by an aria from a rose-breasted grosbeak, a bird which sounds like a robin who has been taking voice lessons.

Most of the guides carry pocket-sized tape recorders with birdsong tapes in place, but they feel that using these to lure birds for the convenience of viewers is unsportsmanlike. Playing the call of a nesting specie heard in distant cover will produce the bird nearby almost instantly as it responds to a territorial challenge. It does seem unfair to confuse and distract the birds using taped calls during this busy breeding and nesting period. The guides are reluctant to use them but sometimes the tiny warblers do all their warbling in faraway treetops and the guide, who has a dozen or more birders crowded around him anxious to see something, feels a real pressure to produce birds. He may punch the button and let the recording artist chirp a few times and then there is always action.

Some of the birds calls are so similar to human phrasing that it is difficult to resist the temptation to identify them by what they sound like. The white-throated sparrow sings, "old Sam Peabody, Peabody." The oven bird calls "teacher, teacher," and the chestnut-sided warbler seems to be saying "Pleased to meetcha." The alder flycatcher orders, "three beers, please," and the barred owl asks, "Who cooks for you?"

Later that morning, crossing over the North Brule River bridge, we all tumble out of the van when guide Dave Benson hears the loud, burbling trill of water thrushes coming from the tangle of alders near the bridge abutments. Most of the members of the warbler family are tiny little birds like the parula, and they flit around in dense foliage near the treetops. But the water thrush is a little larger and more companionable warbler. It feeds and nests near the ground, its velvety brown back and yellow-barred breast make it easy to spot and its almost constant sputtering and hopping around increase its visibility. We lean on the bridge rail, adjusting our field glasses, checking field notes, watching and listening to these bold little busybodies of the riverbanks.

These early June trips in the north always seem to be during prime mosquito time and our van driver, Nancy Waver, passes among us offering sheets of Bounce, the fabric softener, to tuck under our collars and caps to repel the little assassins.

"An old Ojibwe trick," she explains. And it works.

Another reason for the stop at the North Brule River bridge is to check out a three-toed woodpecker cavity in a jack pine at the edge of the parking lot Dave had spotted earlier. This is a bird of the far north forest—very rare here. Only about a dozen sightings have been made in Minnesota in the past several years. A check of the Sibley range maps indicated that the Minnesota/Ontario border is at the extreme southern edge of the territory where this little, yellow-capped woodpecker may be found. Instead of drilling into the tree like other woodpeckers, it uses its bill to chisel off sheets of bark when searching for insects. It usually nests in dead jack pines and it scrapes the bark away from the entrance, so its home is easy to spot as the pale orange trunk wood around the cavity flags its location. This occupant is at home. He hops out, perching at the edge of his doorway while we snap pictures, scribble notes and applaud his performance, thrilled with the sighting of this unusual bird.

Later in the morning we make a detour down to Milepost Five on the Lima Mountain Grade because one of the other groups had reported a good sighting of a great gray owl in that area. No owl for us, but we do have one last great sighting before lunch: a black-billed cuckoo, which is not usually found around here, but they love tent caterpillars and this year's infestation lured the cuckoos in from their usual habitats to the west. On the way back to the lodge we see three moose ambling along the crest of a low, open ridge next to the road. Birding on the Gunflint almost always turns up plenty of wildlife surprises.

The Grand Marais Birding Festival on the Lake Superior North Shore is held in late October during the fall migration period. Species sighted quite regularly include Pacific loons, harlequin ducks, golden eagles, northern mockingbirds, Bohemian waxwings, kittiwakes, king eiders, gyrfalcons and Iceland gulls. The birders sometimes record sightings of such rare species as the ancient murrelet, the purple sandpiper and the ivory gull.

Any prize involves risk, and birding weather on the North Shore in late October can be foul, with howling winds, snow or ice storms and freezing rain. But beautiful autumn weather is just as possible as it was during the first two fall birding festivals in '01 and '02.

"Anything is possible on the North Shore in October," the birders say.

Heading out past the lighthouse, the schooner *Hjordis*, flagship of the North House Folk School, takes daily visitor excursions on Lake Superior. It also serves as a floating classroom for water ecology classes offered by the school.

CHAPTER 11

Grand Marais:
The Shining City on the Hill

Grand Marais, at the head of the Gunflint Trail, is a small town that accents the North Shore of Lake Superior like the golden child in a rather plain family because of the town's striking natural beauty.

Most of Grand Marais' history, charm and ambience comes from the lake and North Shore. There is a spectacular view from the crest of the Sawtooth range of forest-covered ridges which mass over town like green thunderheads. In summer, the spacious harbor is swashed with white sails, red and yellow hulls, multi-colored kayaks, and the tannin colored sails of the North House schooner *Hjordis*. The heavily wooded, stony beaches of Artists' Point are barnacled to the great crabclaw breakwater with its lighthouse, the old Coast Guard Station and the breathtaking expanse of Lake Superior, which has governed and guided the town's destiny for over a century.

The town was named Grand Marais more than 200 years ago by voyageurs because of the Great Harbor...or the Great Marsh? There has been confusion and controversy about that name because in modern French, the word "marais" means swamp or marsh, but in the Old French of the voyageurs who named it, "marais" could mean harbor or refuge. It appears as Grand Marais on the primitive navigation charts of Lake Superior made by 18th century French mapmakers long before there was any organized town. In *Pioneers in the Wilderness*, Raff quotes "the most thoughtful and thorough historian of the voyageurs, Grace Lee Nute" as saying, "A general knowledge of French would lead one to suppose that the words (Grand Marais) meant large swamp. French Canadian voyageurs, however, had their own special vocabulary, in which the word 'Marais' on a coast referred to a harbor, or refuge, or placid cove or bay."

Down the shore forty miles is Little Marais. There is also a Grand Marais, Michigan, on the south shore of Superior, and another on Lake St. Clair near Detroit. All of these towns have natural harbors and no evidence of swamps. For years historians have been lining up behind both positions.

Writing about the Grand Marais name paradox in *The Michigan Academician*, historian Bernard C. Peters of Northern Michigan University examines the history of Grand Marais, Michigan on the south shore of Lake Superior between Whitefish Point and Grand Island. He writes, "Many French names on Lake Superior's shoreline are descriptive of an important landscape feature found at those locations....the places on Lake Superior presently labeled Grand Marais are not, and were not, marshes at all, but critical harbors of refuge for the coasting canoes and bateaux of the voyageurs." Marais definitely means marsh in French, but Peters looks to the original Native American name, *Kitchi-bitobig*, which means "great pond," or place of placid water. That word for pond was rendered in Old French as "mare" by the voyageurs, hence "Grand Mare" was great pond (or harbor).

The first U.S. Postal Service name of the unorganized town of Grand Marais, Minnesota, was "Hiawatha" in 1856, but for some reason, unexplained by history, the post office was closed in 1858, and the name reverted to the old voyageur name of Grand Marais.

In September of 1854, after the Ojibwe had relinquished their claims to all land in northeastern Minnesota, Richard Godfrey and six others—land speculators and prospectors who had started from Duluth—paddled a large birchbark canoe into the harbor and found the area unoccupied except for a few speculators from Detroit. Other than unrecorded early French explorers who named the spot where they found refuge, these were the first white men to settle and build cabins in the Grand Marais area.

Even though they are joined at the hip of Pincushion Mountain, Grand Marais and the Gunflint Trail are two different worlds. They have a "split personality" as Raff indicates. Grand Marais is a city of commerce and has been since 1870 when three ambitious entrepreneurs, Ted Wakelin, Henry Mayhew and Sam Howentstine, gained control of all the real estate in the village including the waterfront. They guessed rightly that whoever controlled the bay would control the town and its business. Raff, in *Pioneers in the Wilderness*, sets the scene:

"By year end of 1873, these three men had secured all the land comprising the original village and all the lands facing the West Bay, as well as the East Bay. Throughout the remainder of the century, they carefully retained control of those valuable properties by means of a confusing tangle of partnerships, court actions and interlocking corporate directorships for the building of general purpose docks, warehouses, railroad rights-of-way, and ore docks."

Those ambitious plans never worked out, but the concept and the work of the three entrepreneurs created a business mission and presence that has remained.

Great Lakes schooners like the 98-foot *Pierpont* and the 63-foot *Charley* were plying Lake Superior by 1860 delivering freight and mail to Grand Marais and other ports. The two-masted, 91-foot, full-sailed brigantine *Columbia* in 1835 was the first ore boat on the lake, carrying copper ore from Michigan and Isle Royale hand loaded onto her decks. Steamers like the *Chippewa*, the *Florence*, the *Swallow*, the sidewheeler *Illinois* and the *Independence* all were part of the busy commercial scene in early Grand Marais.

In *Tales of the Old North Shore*, Howard Sivertson writes, "Boat Day was a cause for celebration in the larger communities on deep water harbors like Grand Marais, where happy citizens, dogs and even a moose would gather to meet the boat." This was the locally famous "snoose moose," who chewed tobacco, met ships and gave sleigh rides in winter.

The period of Grand Marais' greatest economic growth spurt, from 1890 to 1915, prior to its discovery by sportsmen, artists and vacationers, was relatively short, but explosive and consisted primarily of commercial fishing and logging, each of which has left vivid cultural legacies.

Several Grand Marais area art galleries present dramatic scenes of storm-beaten fishing adventures, logging camps and river drives. Local antique stores do a lively business in hand carved and painted net floats and lures, molded net weights, axes, knives and logging chains. Old wooden fishing dories and skiffs rest casually next to business places. Some in yards are used as planters now. Restaurants and markets sell many of the smoked and fresh products of the Big Lake, and down the shore, in Tofte, a museum of commercial fishing has opened to preserve and share the region's commercial fishing heritage.

The wooden *Mackinaw*, built at the North House Folk School, is a working reproduction of a traditional type of boat used on Lake Superior for decades.

Commercial fishing on Lake Superior started in 1823 when John Jacob Astor decided to turn his failing American Fur Company into a commercial fishing venture. Whitefish, lake trout, sturgeon, herring and bluefin were the main products of the lake. With the influx of Norwegian immigrant fishermen in the 1890s, many of them from the province of Stavanger, Grand Marais acquired its colorful Scandinavian character. A Lucia Queen of Lights is selected in early December during *Julefest* at the Bethlehem Lutheran Church, and a very special day, *Syttendenmai,* celebrating Norwegian independence, is observed every May 17. In homes and restaurants fattigman, lefse, spritz cookies, krumkakke, sandbakkels, lutefisk and King Oscar's plum pudding are still served at Christmastime. Even the pizza comes from Sven and Ole's.

They were incredible seamen, those early Scandinavian fishermen, hardy beyond belief and instinctive navigators. Sometimes they used early "one lunger" outboard motors after they were available, but many rowed or sailed in all weather and for great distances. Miles from any visible shore in dense fog, with no radar, sonar, or Global Positioning System, they were able to home in on their nets or a particular reef with only a pocket compass, get their work done and row back to their docks practically in a straight line, often with a stiff nor'easter blowing and spitting sleet. The clouds and the winds, the "feel" of the waves, the activities of shorebirds and other natural indicators were studied carefully every day because their lives depended on being weatherwise.

Families of those hardy adventurers who dared the Big Lake every day in tiny boats still nurture the traditions of the early years. Howard Sivertson, the artist/writer son of a Norwegian fisherman, who as a lad spent many an adventurous day on the lake with his father, has created several superbly illustrated books which recall the days when his family and other hardy adventurers built their cabins in sheltered coves along the rugged shore and on Isle Royale, challenging the Big Lake in tiny boats. He, his wife and daughters—all remarkably gifted artists and gallery owners—have created a visual legacy of Lake Superior's history and grandeur.

Artist and writer Ingeborg Holte, whose father also was a Norwegian commercial fisherman, recalled in her charming memoir, *Ingeborg's Isle Royale*, the joys and fears of a childhood lived on the great island off the North Shore always at the mercy of the moody Lake Superior. These stalwart Scandinavian pioneers settled onto the rocky coves and hills around town and on Isle Royale, wresting their living from the often harsh environment. Now, much of that has changed, but the lure of the North Shore continues and their descendants have never left the Grand Marais area. Anderson, Berglund, Boostrom, Eliason,

Gilbertson, Hanson, Hedstom, Holte, Jacobsen, Johnson, ̶
Nelson, Olson, Pederson and Peterson, Tofte, Toftey Rindahl
some of the pioneer Grand Marais Scandinavian family name
2002 telephone directory.

Commercial and sport fishing boats still leave the harbor every summer morning, but the invasion of the sea lamprey through the St. Lawrence Seaway into all the Great Lakes in 1959 destroyed most of the food fish resource. In *The Superior North Shore*, Thomas F. Waters says this invasion was responsible for "the most profound ecological effect in the history of the lakes." At about the same time, smelt were introduced into the lake, and these ate most of the lake trout spawn, accenting the death knell of the commercial fishing industry. Prior to 1959, millions of pounds of fish were shipped from Grand Marais, nearby Hovland and Tofte to markets all over the country every year. According to Sivertson, the annual herring run alone produced about 10,000 pounds of fish a day.

At one point in the 1890s, so many fish were taken that shoreline pollution became a big problem. In *Pioneers in the Wilderness*, Raff writes:

"Some of the fishermen thoughtlessly dumped enormous quantities of fish guts and rotting bait indiscriminately along the Shore. These garbage dumps were of a magnitude far beyond the disposal efforts of the numerous herring gulls! Indignant citizens protested about the nauseating practice to the town board."

Logging was the economic engine in large part responsible for the early growth of the Grand Marais area, and it didn't take the logging companies much more than twenty years to practically skin the entire northeastern segment of Minnesota of marketable trees before moving west. The logs were brought to Hovland, Tofte and the Grand Marais Harbor by rail, wagon, sleigh and river drives where they were chained into enormous rafts to be towed to Duluth to the largest sawmill on the continent. One sixty-acre raft, described by Raff, was the largest ever afloat on Lake Superior, and contained 5 million board feet of lumber. Towed by the powerful *Gettysburg* tug, the raft was visible in Grand Marais for two days as it passed, and took twelve days to get to Duluth.

Even though most of the big red and white pines that covered the region are gone now, there is still some logging and much heritage. Remnants of the industry are still a significant part of the local economy.

The Hedstrom family of Grand Marais is the typical American success story: hardworking, foresighted Swedish immigrants who provided the much-need-d building lumber in the fast growing pre-World War I economy. The Hedstrom Lumber Company in its early years was a sawmill, but progressively its business included logging, finished lumber, railroad ties, a shingle and box mill, wood chips and a retail home store.

Not an unusual business story perhaps, but it has a typical Grand Marais/Scandinavian flavor. Company ownership has stayed in the same family since its start by Swedish immigrant, Andrew Hedstrom, in 1914. There were 12 Hedstrom children and many of them remained in the family business. Six brothers of the Anderson family were employed at the Hedstrom Mill in the early days and several of their sons have followed them to Hedstrom's. Now the third generation of Hedstroms is involved, making it the oldest company in the state to remain in single family ownership and operation.

It was primarily the twice weekly steamships that brought most of the early tourist business to Grand Marais and the Gunflint region, which continues to be the largest and most lasting infusion of money into the local economy. Over the years, the *Easton*, the *Hiram Dixon*, the *America*, the *Bon Ami* and several others brought tourists, businessmen, cattle, salt, pigs, freight and all manner of life's amenities to the growing city. They would depart loaded with lumber, gravel, fish, berries and potatoes. Most of those steamers are on the bottom of the lake now. The *Dixon* burned at Michipicoten Island in August of 1903, and the *America* hit a submerged bank and sank off Isle Royale on June 28, 1928, but steamers and the later luxury liners, like the *Huronic* and the *North American*, put Grand Marais on the map as a tourist destination.

In his florid style, so popular with newspaper readers of the day, *Cook County Herald* editor, Chris Murphy, wrote in July of 1905:

"Travelers and cruisers are in praise of our climate and golden weather of the North Shore. They say it invigorates the whole system, gives life and strength to the body and energy and renewed activities to the inner man. The excursion season is now underway and every passing boat has its human cargo of hayfever fugitives, pleasure seekers and rest seekers."

At the same time, overland travel also increased in popularity. The road that was to become U.S. Highway 61, the North Shore Drive, opened in 1900 as a four-part stagecoach road: Duluth to Two Harbors, Two Harbors to Silver Bay, Silver Bay to Pork Bay near Caribou Falls, and then on to Grand Marais. Because the road was so rocky and corduroyed with logs, it was a faster trip in winter when sleighs could move more easily over the snow-covered, rugged terrain, but the trip still took several days with three overnight stops. Tourists seemed to feel even then that getting there was half the fun as every sleigh and stage was booked to its nine passenger capacity.

By 1910, there were 80,000 automobiles and 6,000 trucks and buses exploring America's primitive highway system. Prior to World War I, a few Model T Fords and Duryeas were bouncing and rattling up the rugged North Shore Drive, but it wasn't until 1920 that grades were lessened, sharp curves straightened, sturdy bridges built and a stable roadbed established.

Superior's North Shore has always been Grand Marais' premier attraction. A comparison, which is unfair to both regions, is often made to the Coast of Maine. Both are rocky coasts, but their terrain and geology are very different. The Maine coast is a "drowned shore"; that is, it was covered by the ocean before glaciation, which resulted in hundreds of fjords, inlets, salt marshes, long bays and hidden coves creating a very irregular, indented shoreline. There, river valleys became bays and hills became islands, as opposed to the almost solid wall of rampart-like cliffs of volcanic origin which characterize Superior's North Shore.

In 1893, a Norwegian immigrant and commercial fisherman, Ole Brunes, had added 6 rooms onto his house in nearby Hovland—the next town up the shore from Grand Marais. Hovland had become known as the "Trout Capital of the World," and Brunes expanded his house to accommodate sport fishermen. He also built a tourist cabin at the mouth of the Flute Reed River that same year. Also in '93, C.A.A. Nelson, a Swede born in Norkoping, Ostergotland, opened a similar "resort" in his home at Lutsen, a short ways down the Shore, which has operated continuously since that time. Nelson named the resort and the town to memorialize the death of the Swedish king, Gustavus Adolphus, killed in the Battle of Lutzen in 1830 in Saxony, West Germany.

Brunes and Nelson on the North Shore near Grand Marais, and Hans Gilbertson on the Gunflint Trail, with his moose hunter shacks on the South Brule River and Assinika Creek in 1897, were the first "resorters" and the earliest pioneers of the tourist industry in the region. Tourism has grown every year since, especially since winter activities such as ice fishing, cross country skiing, winter camping and snowmobiling have extended the season by several months.

As the bright jewel along the North Shore, Grand Marais seemed the only logical location for an extraordinary enterprise called the North House Folk School. The concept of the folk school, or *folkhogskole*, originated in Denmark in the mid-19th century by Bishop Nicolai Gundvig as an inter-generational, lifelong learning experience. The idea quickly spread to Norway where there are now 82 folk schools. North House in Grand Marais was started in 1997 and offers year-round courses in Scandinavian craft traditions, fiber arts, birchbark weaving, timber frame building, wooden boat building, freshwater studies on the schooner *Hjordis*, blacksmithing, folk arts such as Scandinavian flat plane carving and many others.

The school emphasizes natural materials and northern living, issues no grades and offers a noncompetitive method of education that features interaction between instructor and students. Their mission statement promises "promoting and preserving the knowledge, skills and crafts of the past and the present." It is in an informal partnership with the city of Grand Marais, which supplied the site and the buildings, and is one of four Folk Schools in the country.

One of the new course offerings at North House includes artisan bread baking, during which the construction of the brick ovens the bread is baked in is taught. One of their first courses was coffin building, which may have been inspired by a request Helmer Aakvik made of Mark Hansen, a Grand Marais boat builder, several years before Hansen became the first director of North House.

Aakvik, the legendary, indestructible, prototypical Norwegian commercial fisherman, who survived many near-death experiences on the Big Lake over the years, stopped at Hansen's place one day and asked Mark if he could build a coffin for him. Surprised, Mark asked him if he wasn't feeling well.

"Oh, yah, I'm feeling pretty good," said Helmer. "But I'm over 80, you know, and you gotta think about these things."

"Well, sure Helmer, I guess I could do that," replied Mark.

"Oh, and one more thing, Mark," Aakvik asked. "Could you build it shaped like my fishing boat?

Mark thought for a moment and then said, "Yeah, Helmer, I believe I could do that. I'll have to come out to your place and do some measuring and get a good look at it though. Maybe take a couple pictures of it."

"Fine, come on out any time," said Helmer.

Mark got all the necessary supplies, got to work on Helmer's coffin modeled after his sixteen-foot skiff, and had it done in a few weeks, not knowing when it might be needed. Helmer thought it was great and hauled it to his home up the shore.

A couple years went by and Helmer was still pretty spry. One day they met in Grand Marais.

"Well, Helmer," Mark inquired, "Is the coffin still OK?"

"Oh, it's great, Mark," Helmer replied. "I sleep in it every night. It's real comfortable."

A passion for the visual arts has always flourished in Grand Marais as it has in most areas of natural grandeur. The New England coast, California's Big Sur, the Florida Keys, the desert southwest and the Rocky Mountains are but a few of these regions which, like Superior's North Shore, have become meccas for artists. All forms of genre art have been the defining trademark of Grand Marais for a century.

It all started with Anna Johnson, wife of the frenetic entrepreneur, Charlie Johnson, who was postmaster, logger, fur trader, ore hauler, retail merchant, road builder, land speculator, banker, county treasurer and commissioner, mayor, treasurer of the Cook County Manufacturing Company and sawmill owner, and who kept many of these balls in the air at the same time, yet always managed to be an active patron of the arts.

Anna Carolina Johnson, his second cousin, was born in the Swedish town of Arvika, as was Charlie, and emigrated to Michigan in 1891. They were married in Chicago on April 3, 1907 and according to Raff in *Pioneers in the Wilderness*:

"Anna began immediately to broaden her work in watercolors and etchings particularly in interpreting scenes along the North Shore, in Grand Marais and up the Gunflint Wagon Road; a modern critic would note striking similarity between her fine-line, exacting realism and the technique later refined by Andrew Wyeth. Anna successfully experimented with leather, tissue paper and wax. And she produced many delicately painted ceramic and china pieces which she fired in her own kiln."

Early on, Anna began art workshops for young painters, was a promoter of the arts in Grand Marais, and Raff, among others, traces her influence to the establishment of Grand Marais' reputation as an art colony. The Johnson Heritage Post, the architectural centerpiece of the downtown—a beautiful log art gallery—is a memorial to Anna Johnson and her dedication to the arts. Much of her remaining work is featured in one wing of the building.

Another dominating figure in the development of Grand Marais' pre-eminence as an art center was Birney Quick, who founded the Grand Marais Art Colony in the summer of 1947 in association with the Minneapolis School of Art. The summer classes, according to Jay Anderson, former executive director of the Colony, "were intended to be a fast track in art skills for returning [World War

II] veterans."

The Colony, which grew rapidly, maintains a membership of about 200, has its own building, sponsors the Grand Marais Arts Festival and a biennial, two-week art workshop in Tuscany and Umbria in "the green heart of Italy." The colony also holds ten workshops each summer in Grand Marais for adults from intermediate to advanced as well as young and intergenerational artists, many of whom crowd the town all summer.

About the adult workshops, Anderson says, "They last a full week and are designed more for the intermediate to advanced emerging artists rather than the beginner. As a result the workshops are less 'instructional' or media specific and are designed more to help the artist explore or discover his or her own personal voice. We do offer workshops in print making and Sumi-e, as well as life drawing, but again the atmosphere is more one of student-mentor than student-instructor." Anderson, an articulate enthusiast of natural settings for learning and producing great art, says of the Colony location:

"Certainly with the wilderness at our back door and Lake Superior at our front, Grand Marais has become a haven for artists, writers and performers wishing to create in a more pristine environment than they might otherwise find in the state. The energy they derive, however is not just a reflection of what they see set down on canvas or paper. The place seems to be absorbed into the artists and presented back to the viewer through the filter of their own experiences and interaction with this magical place. Perhaps that is the fundamental difference between 'pictures' and 'paintings.'"

The Grand Marais Playhouse, named by *Minnesota Monthly* magazine as "the best outstate theater in Minnesota," is now in its 32nd season. "Drama has no stigma in Grand Marais. Even the football players try out when we audition for a Shakespeare play," says Sue Hennessy, the ebullient Production Manager, who oversees 23 productions a year. Hennessy, who brings to her work at the Playhouse experience on Broadway and at Minneapolis' Guthrie Theater, is thrilled about the ten-day annual Shakespeare Festival. For this project, the Playhouse is partnering with the Minnesota Shakespeare Project, which hopes to make Grand Marais its permanent summer home. Like most Grand Marais arts activities, the Playhouse has solid area support, with hundreds subscribing to the year-round schedule of plays, including the several they produce each year in the school system.

There are also innovative groups like the comedy improv Flying Leap, which has several national appearances on its calendar, and Sterling Dance, a very active dance company in its eighth season. Several musical groups offer a variety of instrumental and vocal program content from Bach to rock at concerts throughout the year. Several arts groups' offices, performing space, galleries and also community radio studios are headquartered in the new Arrowhead Center for the Arts wing of the new high school building.

That such a superabundance of cultural activities should be thriving in a small town at the edge of Minnesota's wilderness is truly remarkable and it provides a certain classiness to the community and the surrounding area. This emphasis on the arts in Grand Marais engenders generous and energetic support from government, business, institutions, foundations and economic development agencies.

There is some apprehension in Grand Marais about a tourist economy that has subtly changed the town and a fear that control of the city's destiny may shift from local to outside control. This is a very common problem among communities with tourist attractions across the nation, but seems to be most intense in those with very little support from their original economies or close to extinction due to location and transportation problems.

In *Devil's Bargain*, his book about how a tourist economy changes a community, Hal Rothman says "...because tourism often results in a redistribution of wealth and power to 'outsiders,' it represents a new form of colonialism for the region." There is often grumbling heard about tourists and outsiders taking over the town, but except for the retired population and a faltering logging industry, residents are largely dependent on the direct or secondary circulation of tourist dollars. With its shimmering setting and unique character, Grand Marais has been easing into a tourist-dominated economy for 80 years and will be a major player in the state's vacation travel industry for years to come.

Boats of every description from schooners to kayaks pull into the gaily decorated Grand Marais harbor filling the shops, parks and restaurants with visitors who pump the life blood of tourist dollars into the economies of all North Shore communities.

In some ways, the Cross River in the Round Lake area is a window looking into the future of the Gunflint region because it is timeless. It is short and swift, has no buildings or evidence of any habitation on it. It is completely a wild river. Other than the temporary disturbance of storm-damaged trees, it is probably exactly the same as it was thousands of years ago. With the care and concern of the people who love The Gunflint, it will probably remain forever wild.

Afterword

Researching the past and present cultural and natural history of a region creates an irresistible urge to speculate, to attempt looking into the future. What are things going to be like here on The Gunflint in 50 years? 100 years?

The help I needed with this inquiry would have to come from a futurist, someone with horizons in his eyes who could examine the past, synthesize pertinent knowledge and make some educated guesses about what the coming century might hold in store for this unique region.

Dave Zumeta, executive director of the Minnesota Forest Council, was just the person I was looking for. Zumeta has spent most of his professional life planning the future of Minnesota's natural resources, including time spent as head of forest planning for Minnesota's Department of Natural Resources and as their liaison to both the Chippewa and Superior National Forests. He worked for several years on the Governor's Smart Growth Initiative, which attempted to evaluate and influence Minnesota's growth, development and lifestyle requirements for years into the future

"What is it going to be like here on The Gunflint?" I asked him. "What are going to be the major influences on our future?"

Staring at a large Superior National Forest map on his wall and ticking his responses off on his fingers he replied without hesitation: "Demographics and population changes; the possibility of global warming; 'popple' farming and the Internet. Those four things are going to shape The Gunflint's future."

Having witnessed population changes over the past several years I told him about my recent visit to the State Demographer's office for population data, and discovered that Cook County had a greater growth rate than any other northern county in the past ten years. Why?

"Because it is amenity rich," he sated in planner's language. "That means that it is such a great place, has so many amenities, that a lot of people want to live there or have second homes there. Especially the retiring baby boomers and elderly people, both of whom have considerable disposable incomes."

Zumeta went on to discuss "popple farming," a method of cultivating fast-growing aspen trees as a farm row crop, which would greatly affect forest logging because of the reduction of equipment, transportation and labor costs. He mentioned that Champion International Paper was already raising these hybrid aspen on a 2,500-acre plot near Alexandria and were expecting eight-inch-diameter trees in a few years for the production of paper and strandboard.

"The long term effect in the northeastern part of the state will be that large scale aspen logging in forestland will probably be a thing of the past," Zumeta continued. "These aspen farms will likely be in the northwest and central parts of the state and possibly in major river bottom areas in flat, poorly drained land that is ideally suited to raising poplars and where there are farmers who have the land, the mindset, business sense and equipment to get involved in productive, viable farming operations."

"Much of the forestland land will become far too valuable as recreational property to tie up in growing commercial timber. In northern Minnesota we have already seen that happening and it is going to increase. With homesteading votes these new property owners will likely exert a lot of pressure on the U.S. Forest Service, the Minnesota DNR and county land commissioners to manage the land for recreation rather than for timber production.

"In the future I think one of the biggest attractions is going to be the water," he went on. "If we do experience any of the greenhouse warming effect, it will probably get warmer and drier to the south, and there is going to be less and less water. Lake Superior, the largest area of fresh water in the world, is going to provide clean water and cool temperatures, some things that may be very short in other areas of the country. Lake Superior, that big ice box, is going to be very attractive."

That led us to a discussion about the possibilities of global warming, or the greenhouse effect, which would increase the carbon dioxide content of the atmosphere. Zumeta referred me to the research on the subject of global warming that has been done at the University of Minnesota's Department of Forest Resources and the University of Minnesota Duluth's Natural Resources Research Institute.

Dr. Margaret Davis, the distinguished Regents Professor of Ecology at the

University of Minnesota, explained the ground rules for looking at her publication on changes in the northern Minnesota forest under certain conditions of climate change in which the carbon dioxide content of the atmosphere was increased.

Using computerized models, which input climate tolerances per specie, and which use a number of climate controls to predict the distribution of trees, Dr. Davis has attempted to project the future distribution of each forest specie.

"These models are not designed for details," Dr. Davis cautions. "They are more general. They portray the forest in ten year segments. The shorter the time, the more accurate the map will be, but you must remember, climate cannot be predicted on a fine scale. How fast can you move a forest? It is very misleading to try to simplify these maps just for public consumption."

The results of this carbon dioxide increase over 90 years that show up on Dr. Davis' maps are a displacement to the north of the boreal forest species we are so familiar with: pines, cedars, spruces, and their replacement by deciduous, hardwood trees as the climate moderates. The profile of the land and the forest would likely remain much the same, but as one ecologist told me, "The BWCAW will probably look more like Robin Hood's Sherwood Forest with white oaks, maples, ash, aspen and maybe cottonwoods predominating."

If this happened, the wooded, hilly area just north of the Superior shore could open up into savannas and fields and we would see a resurgence of an agricultural economy.

In his book, *Minnesota's Natural Heritage*, ecologist John Tester suggests that this part of the Arrowhead might look much as it did before World War I during which time those south facing slopes along the lake became farm country after being laid bare by logging.

Cultural history usually follows land use and when the trees were all logged off and the slash burned, the land was plowed and planted with corn, alfalfa hay, barley and potatoes. In M. J. Humphrey's *Pioneer Faces and Places*, there is a photograph of Tom Parent and W.C. Smith standing in a corn field near Schroeder where the cornstalks are over their heads and another photo of loaded wagons during harvest time at Hovland.

Livestock was also common in the area as the July 15, 1913, issue of the Grand Marais Herald informed citizens of the recently passed Ordinance No.17 "This is the last day of freedom for bulls, horses and pigs in Grand Marais. Ordinance No. 17 restraining such animals from running at large is published in this issue of the Herald, and thus becomes law. Owners are warned that the ordinance is to be strictly enforced and that therefore, it will be an economy to keep all stock off the streets. And if the cows continue to show a preference for pasturing on the sidewalks it is only a matter of time before they will have to be classed with horses, bulls and pigs and have their liberties curtailed by the ordinance also."

In the past the Gunflint region contained only a cabin-dwelling remote society. The first ones here were prospectors, land speculators and a merchant group supplying these efforts. Then came the trappers, loggers and farmers. Then resorters, canoe outfitters, tourists, sportsmen and retirees. Now it is second home owners and a rapidly growing computer technology oriented group of business owners working out of year-round homes. Brokers, marketers, designers, executive and technical search firms, financial services, web site preparation—all these businesses and more are beginning to appear in cabins and homes on forest roads that used to see an occasional boat and trailer, but now are on the regular route of UPS and FedEx trucks. In an article in the St. Paul Pioneer Press, entitled "Little Office in the Woods," staff writer Dennis Lien says, "From the outside, the lake homes may look the same. But inside they are workspaces for a set of plugged-in high speed newcomers."

The slogan of the computer generation—a group one news magazine called the "wired loners"—who have been moving into the Gunflint region is "Remoteness is Irrelevant."

The Internet seems made for remote environments and this is spawning a new population with different lifestyles, a new language and little sophistications, which are drawing the area slowly but inexorably away from its rustic origins. The needs and wants of this new groups will require new services and amenities, which will bring another economic boost to the area.

That seems to be one of the scenarios the future is offering the Gunflint region: climate and population changes and new occupations from new technologies. These new directions will bring new opportunities and a surging economy to the North Shore in general and Grand Marais in particular. In the near future are a new marina in a federally funded Safe Harbor, which will be utilized by greater recreational use of Lake Superior, a proposed community arts college, a new Trailhead for the Gunflint, new medical facilities, new retail establishments, restaurants and accommodations.

There may be some changes in vegetation, population, water levels and wildlife, but The Gunflint hasn't changed all that much in the past 100 years, and it probably will not change much more in the coming century as long as it remains entirely within the boundaries of the Superior National Forest from Maple Hill to Saganaga.

Over Pincushion Mountain and on up the Trail the bounty of nature and the spiritual enrichment that author Paul Gruchow called "the grace of the wild," will likely remain. Here is a vestige of an earlier America in its unique, jewel-like, northwoods setting, confined by an inland sea, a roadless canoe wilderness, a national forest and an international boundary. A healing place, the kind Jill Nelson referred to in *Essays on the Last Great Places* as "a place where Nature and human nature conspire to make survival possible."

This young black bear, probably a three-year-old cub, stopped at Henricksson's Gunflint cabin most summer days for a refreshing drink from the hummingbird feeder on the front deck.

About the Author

John Henricksson was the director of publicity (Tourism) for the State of Minnesota from 1952–1962 and has written environmental, outdoor and travel news and features for newspapers, magazines and TV for thirty years. He headed a public relations agency for ten years which focused on outdoor recreational products and services. He was selected to write the young reader's biography of Rachel Carson for the "12 Americans Who Have Made a Difference" series.

He is the editor of *Northwriters: A Strong Woods Collection*, *Northwriters: Our Place in the Woods*, and the author of *A Wild Neighborhood*, which was illustrated by Betsy Bowen. Both Henricksson and Bowen won Minnesota Book Awards in the Nature Writing and Illustration category for *A Wild Neighborhood*. All of these books were published by University of Minnesota Press.

Henricksson divides his time between his home in Mahtomedi, Minnesota, and his Gunflint Lake cabin.

CPSIA information can be obtained
at www.ICGtesting.com
Printed in the USA
JSHW041429070421
13371JS00001B/13